W9-BDG-903

MODERN WORLD NATIONS

Nepal

Krishna P. Bhattarai

Series Editor
Charles F. Gritzner
South Dakota State University

An imprint of Infobase Publishing

Frontispiece: Flag of Nepal

Cover: Patan Durbar Square, Nepal

Nepal

Copyright © 2008 by Infobase Publishing

Chelsea House
An imprint of Infobase Publishing
132 West 31st Street
New York NY 10001

Library of Congress Cataloging-in-Publication Data

Bhattarai, Krishna P.
  Nepal / Krishna P. Bhattarai.
    p. cm. — (Modern world nations)
  Includes bibliographical references and index.
  ISBN 978-0-7910-9672-7 (hardcover)
  1. Nepal—Juvenile literature. I. Title. II. Series.

  DS493.4.B495 2008
  954.96—dc22   2008002980

Chelsea House books are available at special discounts when purchased in bulk quantities for businesses, associations, institutions, or sales promotions. Please call our Special Sales Department in New York at (212) 967-8800 or (800) 322-8755.

You can find Chelsea House on the World Wide Web at http://www.chelseahouse.com

Series design by Takeshi Takahashi
Cover design by Jooyoung An

Printed in the United States of America

Bang NMSG 10 9 8 7 6 5 4 3 2 1

This book is printed on acid-free paper.

All links and Web addresses were checked and verified to be correct at the time of publication. Because of the dynamic nature of the Web, some addresses and links may have changed since publication and may no longer be valid.

Table of Contents

MODERN WORLD NATIONS

Nepal

1

Introducing Nepal

"Mother and Motherland are dearer than the heavens."

—NEPAL'S MOTTO

Nepal is a fascinating and mysterious land that awaits discovery. The country was almost completely closed off to the outside world until the 1950s. As a result, Nepal remains undiscovered and little known to most Westerners even today. Yet those visitors who have discovered this small country tucked away between India and China are overwhelmed by its physical grandeur and the charming diversity of its people. Packed within its borders are the planet's most majestic mountains, the Himalayas. The range includes towering Mount Everest, which, with an elevation of more than 29,000 feet (8,840 meters), is the world's highest peak. In fact, about one-third of Nepal is dominated by the rugged, dramatic peaks of the Himalayas. The Nepalese have a deep affection for their mountains. The peaks also serve as a magnet for adventurers and mountaineers who are lured by their awesome size and beauty.

Culturally, few places in the world of comparable size can match Nepal's diversity. It is a country in which multilingual and multicultural societies are as diverse as its varied natural landscapes. More than 40 different ethnic groups exist within its 56,827 square-mile (147,181 square-kilometer) territory, and about 70 different languages are spoken. These numbers become more meaningful when one realizes that Nepal is about the size of Alabama, or the combined area of Canada's New Brunswick and Nova Scotia.

Nepal's cultural diversity stems from several ancient migrations into the territory. They include Indo-Aryans from the southwest, Tibeto-Burmans from the north, and Dravidians from the south. The country also is the homeland of the Siddhartha Gautama (Gautama Buddha), the founder of Buddhism, one of the world's great religions. This small and hospitable country has become a popular destination for people seeking spiritual enlightenment and peace. Of course, some adventurers also come in search of the elusive Yeti, the legendary "Abominable Snowman" that is said to prowl the high mountains.

Geographically, Nepal is situated on the lap of the Himalayas, in southern Asia. It is bound by the Tibetan Autonomous Region (China) to the north, and by India to the east, south, and west. The country shares a 746-mile (1,200-kilometer) boundary with China and 1,119 miles (1,800 kilometers) with India. Roughly rectangular in shape, Nepal extends about 550 miles (885 kilometers) from east to west and about 120 miles (193 kilometers) north to south. It is one of the world's landlocked countries and lacks a water route to the sea.

Despite being relatively small and completely landlocked, Nepal still has many unique characteristics. Few countries in

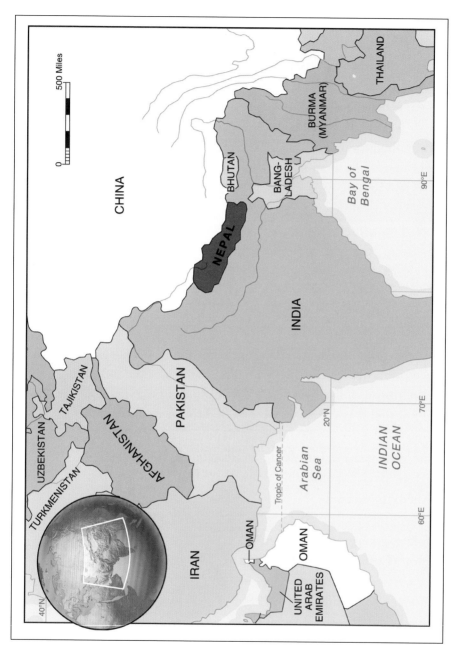

Nepal is located in southern Asia, bounded by the Tibet region of China to the north and India on the south, east, and west. The country covers an area of 56,827 square miles (147,181 square kilometers), and is approximately the size of Alabama.

the world, for example, can match its tremendous diversity in terrain, climate, people, and culture—particularly within a comparable area. Whereas its land features include the world's highest mountain peaks, terrain also plunges to an elevation of less than 200 feet (60 meters) in the far southeast. Because of location and differences in elevation, climatic conditions range from subtropical in the south to polar ice cap atop high mountain peaks. South Asia's famous monsoons bring summer rains that account for about 90 percent of the country's annual precipitation.

Despite its relatively small size and rugged terrain, Nepal is home to nearly 29 million people. This gives the country a whopping population density of about 510 people per square mile (about 200 per square kilometer). With so much of the country unsettled because of terrain, the density is several times higher in those areas where people actually live. Nepal faces a number of challenges as it tries to meet the needs of its booming population. The country's economy is among the poorest in the world. There is little industry, and most people continue to practice subsistence agriculture in an economy that depends heavily upon barter. Nepal's landlocked condition and rugged terrain combine to make transportation linkages inadequate and costly to build. A history of political instability and rampant corruption also are major constraints against development. Consequently, many of the country's potential resources—including abundant water and scenery that could attract tourists—remain relatively undeveloped.

Recently, Nepal experienced extreme political turmoil, including an attempted takeover by Maoists (Communists). Rapid population growth, a stagnant economy, and mounting frustrations combine to make Nepal a very difficult country to govern successfully. Currently, the country is undergoing a governmental transition. Regardless of the outcome, those in power will face many challenges. They must somehow meet the rising expectations of an increasingly impatient population.

Nepalese want adequate incomes, access to resources, better education and health services, and equal opportunity. As this book goes to press, an interim government is in control. It has scheduled elections (which have been delayed on several occasions) to form an assembly, and seeks to create a new and stable federal republic.

People and culture in the northern and southern parts of Nepal tend to resemble those of neighboring regions—China, Tibet, and India. The origin of the name *Nepal* depends on several ancient mythical and historical stories. Many people who inhabit northern Nepal are descendents of people from Tibet. The Tibetan people lived a nomadic lifestyle, herding sheep and producing wool for their livelihood. In the Tibetan language, *ne* means "wool," and *pal* means "house." Therefore, Tibetan people called the Himalayan region *Nepal* in recognition of its wool production.

Similarly, however, the Newar (inhabitants of the Kathmandu Valley) had the word *Nepa,* meaning "country of the middle zone." Because their homeland was situated in the central part of the Himalayas, they called it *Nepal.* Lepcha people, on the other hand, use the word *Nepal* in reference to a "sacred or holy cave." According to yet another story, Manjushri (a Buddhist deity) drained the water from Nagadaha (a mythical lake that is believed to have occupied the Kathmandu Valley). When drained, the valley became inhabitable. According to legend, the valley was ruled by Bhuktaman, a cow herder, under the guidance of a sage named Ne. Because the sage had taken care to rule the sacred country, the land was named *Nepal.* In this version, *Ne* recognizes the name of the sage, and *pal* refers to "taking care." Clearly, the origin of the country's name is subject to wild speculation and is anyone's guess.

Religion plays a very important role in Nepalese society. More than 80 percent of the country's people follow Hinduism or Buddhism, and many Nepalese follow both faiths. Lumbini is the birthplace of Gautama Buddha; hence, it is the home of

Lumbini, a small village near the Indian border, is one of Nepal's most famous locations. Widely believed to be the birthplace of Buddha, Lumbini has become a sacred site to Buddhists all over the world.

Buddhism. Hinduism also took root in Nepal long before the dawn of the Christian era. In addition, Christianity and Islam are widely practiced faiths. Thus, Nepal has great religious diversity. Nepalese respect all religions, and the country has never experienced a religious conflict. A caste system is a deeply entrenched trait of Nepalese culture. Each family in Nepalese society is a member (by birth) of a certain caste, and everyone has to abide by the rules of one's own caste. (The caste system is discussed in Chapter 4.)

Today, Nepal is experiencing rapid—and, in most respects, highly positive—changes. Since 1990, the country has enjoyed a relatively stable democratic government. The result has been widespread improvements in education, communications, transportation, technology, the arts, and water resource development. Tourism also has experienced considerable development during recent years.

In terms of international relations, Nepal has long played the geopolitical role of a strategic buffer zone that has contributed to trans-Himalayan political stability. Located between two antagonistic neighbors, China and India, Nepal has often had a difficult time balancing its relations with the two countries. This was particularly true during periods of conflict within the region. Outside pressures, for example, pressed upon Nepal like a giant vice during the China-India War (1962) and during the Cold War between the West and the Communist world during much of the latter half of the twentieth century.

Diplomatic relationships between Nepal and the United States were established in April 1947, earlier than with either of its neighbors (India in 1947 and China in 1955). The relationship was strained much of the time, however, because of Nepal's own political instability. After the attack on New York's World Trade Center and the Pentagon in Washington, DC, on September 11, 2001, things changed. The United States began to provide technical (military) and other support to the government of Nepal to fight the terrorism being inflicted on the country by Maoist insurgents. The U.S. secretary of state, Colin Powell, visited Nepal and offered his country's support to Nepal's own war against Maoist terrorism. They also discussed human rights, military activities, and development strategies. Relationships between the two countries continue to strengthen. In 2007, for example, Nepal ranked thirteenth among foreign countries with regard to the number of students studying in the United States.

Between 1996 and the signing of a "comprehensive peace agreement" in 2006, Nepal was nearly brought to its knees by a bitter civil conflict. An insurgency led by Maoists (Communist sympathizers) gave the government a list of 40 demands related to issues of nationalism, democracy, and livelihood. The government, of course, sought to put down the rebellion. The result was a very dark period in Nepalese history, one marked by terrible destruction and bloodshed. The "People's War" did, however, have at least one positive effect: People began to think in terms of their well-being and that of their country. Of particular importance, they began to become more aware of the need for greater human rights. They also began to speak out against corruption, feudalism, and monarchism, which had strangled the country's potential for so long.

During recent years, change has come fast and furiously. In 2006, the reinstated Parliament removed the king as the head of state and supreme commander in chief of the Royal Nepalese Army. It also shrank the annual budget and declared that the future status of the monarchy would be decided by the Constituent Assembly. The word *royal* was washed from all official signboards and letter pads across the country. Parliament declared Nepal a secular state, one recognizing the separation of organized religion and government. Unexpectedly, Nepal suddenly appeared a much different country to the rest of the world—and even to the Nepalese. A new buoyancy and atmosphere of optimism began to spread throughout the country.

2

Physical Landscapes

P hysical features and conditions dominate the geography of
Nepal, perhaps to a greater degree than any other elements—
natural or human. Among these features, none dominates in
a more overwhelming way than the country's spectacular mountains
and valleys.

LAND FEATURES AND REGIONS

Nepal's terrain resembles a three-step stairway. In the south, the
land is dominated by a low-lying, relatively flat plain. Farther north,
the plains merge with hills and scattered valleys. The northern one-
third (roughly) of the country is dominated by the world's mightiest
mountain range, the majestic Himalayas.

Geographically, Nepal can be divided into three broad regions:
Terai, hill, and mountain (Himalayas). Each zone stretches in an

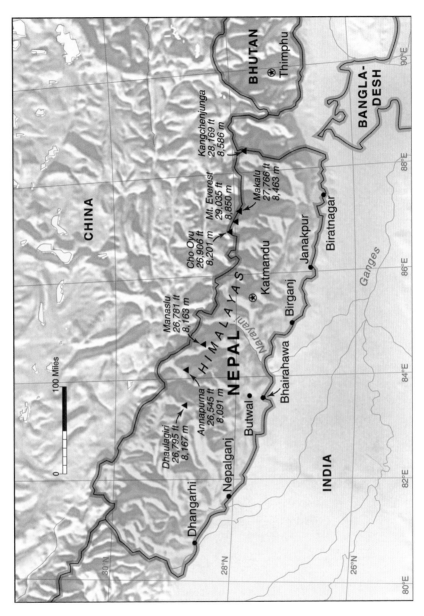

Nepal is divided into three topographical zones: the Terai, the Hill, and the Himalayas. Considered the world's best destination for mountaineering, Nepal contains eight of the ten highest mountains in the world, including Mount Everest at 29,035 feet (8,850 meters) and Kachenjunga at 28,209 feet (8,598 meters), the world's tallest and third tallest, respectively.

east–west direction across the country and differs from the others in many ways. From south to north, they appear as a series of giant steps that rise toward the heavens. Because of marked differences in terrain and elevation, climatic conditions differ from zone to zone. With their different climates, they present a variety of ecosystems, including a wide range of plant and animal life, soils, and so forth. They also differ in terms of natural resources and land use practices. The government uses these regional divisions for planning and administration development. Doing so helps to ensure that all parts of the country are included in various development programs.

Terai Region

The Terai region is the southernmost strip of Nepal. It is bordered by India in the south and by the Mahabharat foothills to the north. Initially, this low-lying plains region was covered with dense, subtropical forests. Today, much of the forest is gone. This is Nepal's most densely populated region and also its most productive agricultural area. Malaria, which once made the Terai all but uninhabitable, has been nearly eradicated. This is the country's breadbasket. Paddy rice, corn (maize), millet, potatoes, mustard, and wheat are major foods crops. Primary cash crops include sugarcane, jute, tea, and bamboo.

Hill Region

Moving northward, the central (east–west) strip is called the hill region. It is formed by the Mahabharat chain, a range of low, rounded hills that reach elevations of approximately 6,500 to 9,500 feet (2,000 to 3,000 meters). The hills are extensively terraced, giving them a striking staircase appearance. Rice is the primary crop raised on terraced land, although wheat, maize, and tea also are grown. Some animals are raised, in addition to crops, and the region also includes popular recreational centers. The south-facing slopes are more densely populated and agriculturally productive than those with a northern exposure; this is because they receive more direct rays of the sun as well as more rainfall.

The hill region includes several valleys and plateaus. Of the valleys lying within the Mahabharat range, none is more important than the Kathmandu Valley. Located in the central part of the country, the valley is the site of Nepal's ancient, historic capital city, Kathmandu.

Mountain Region

The mountain region, formed by the Himalayas, stretches across the northernmost part of the country. It is bordered by the Mahabharat range to the south and by the Tibetan Plateau—the "Roof of the World"—to the north. The mountain region, which ranges from about 6,500 to 29,035 feet (2,000 to 8,850 meters), includes 8 of the world's 10 highest peaks. Most of the region is covered with permanent snowfields, resulting in very little vegetation, population, or economic activity. Hence, Nepal's physiography has been further divided into six regions based on the standard altitudinal divisions. Major portions of the trans-Himalayan lie in the western part of the mountain region of Nepal.

The Himalayas: Where Earth Meets Sky

Himalaya means "abode of snow" in the Sanskrit language. According to the Hindu epic *Mahabharata,* the towering ice and snow-mantled range is a sacred and holy place. It is occupied by Lord Shiva, who married the princess of one of the Himalayan kingdoms. Many Hindu religious books mention visits from gods and goddesses to the Himalayan region on different occasions. This emphasizes the holiness of the Himalayas to those of the Hindu faith, and it strengthens the respect they hold for the mountains. Today, the range still holds mystical and sacred importance to various peoples. Yet it is the awesome dimensions and natural beauty of the Himalayas—range upon range, tier after tier of rocks with their sky-piercing, snow-capped peaks and deep canyons—that most attract visitors from around the world.

According to geologists, the Himalayas are Earth's youngest folded mountains. In fact, they are still in the process of formation; the mountains continue to move northward, and they are still growing in height. To understand their origin, imagine a gigantic bulldozer slamming into southern Asia. What would be the result? You guessed it—a huge pile of rock! *Plate tectonics* refers to the movement of huge chunks of Earth's crust across the planet's surface. Originally, the Himalaya range was uplifted due to the collision of a huge plate—the land that is today the Indian "subcontinent"—with what was then southern Asia. It started during the tertiary period of geologic history, which began about 65 million years ago, and ended at the beginning of the Ice Age, approximately 2 million years ago. This is a very recent event in geologic time, and the mountain-building process continues today.

The Himalayas that stretch beyond Nepal encompass territory of northern India, southern China, Bhutan, northern Pakistan, and northeastern Afghanistan. The total east–west length covers about 1,550 miles (2,400 kilometers) and an area of about 38,460 square miles (100,000 square kilometers) in South Asia. The Nepal Himalayas (about 750 miles, 1,210 kilometers) are located in the central portion of the range. Here, within the country, are seven peaks that reach above 26,246 feet (8,000 meters), including the giant of them all, Mount Everest. No other country can match this spectacular terrain.

These magnificent Himalayan ranges have given Nepal a gift of splendid landscapes, where visitors can also explore not only the mountains but also ancient temples and other cultural resources. Thousands are drawn to the country and its environmental riches each year. These riches include 10 World

Heritage Sites (listed here), 8 of which are located at elevations above 2,000 feet (610 meters):

1. Sagarmatha National Park

2. Patan Durbar Square

3. Kathamandu Durbar Square

4. Bhaktapur Durbar Square

5. Pashupatinath Temple

6. Changu Narayan Temple

7. Swayambhunath Stupa

8. Bouddhanath Stupa

9. Chitwan National Park

10. Lumbini (birthplace of Lord Buddha)

The last two sites are located in southern Terai, or the lowland belt, at an elevation below 2,000 feet (610 meters). The sites include both natural and cultural features of importance. Sagarmatha and Chitwan national parks are natural heritage sites, whereas the other eight are sites based on the country's rich cultural heritage. Conveniently, 7 of the 10 sites are located in or near (within about 20 miles, or 32 kilometers) the Kathmandu Valley.

The Khumbu Region and Mount Everest

Mount Everest—called *Sagarmatha* in the Nepali language (*Chomolungma* in Tibetan)—rises 29,035 feet (8,848 meters) above sea level. The magnificent peak certainly earns the title "Goddess of the Sky." Many of its secrets remained shrouded in mystery until 1953. In that year, a Nepalese Sherpa named Tenzing Norgay and New Zealand adventurer, explorer, and mountaineer

Surrounded by a national park, the tallest peak in the world—Mount Everest—is located in Nepal. Nepal is a small country, and the towering Himalayan mountain range occupies its territory, blessing Nepal with eight of the world's highest peaks.

Edmund P. Hillary became the first people to scale Everest. They reached the summit on May 29 of that year, climbing their way into history and immortality.

Once scaled, Mount Everest soon became a popular challenge for trekkers and mountaineers from around the world. Many visitors, of course, came simply to view the snow- and ice-capped peaks that resemble sparkling white pyramids reaching for the heavens. The Khumbu region, home of the Sherpa people, is also a popular Himalayan destination that welcomes the trekkers with its Sherpa hospitality. Sherpa—known as the "Snow Leopards"—are the world's best-known mountain climbers. They also are the skilled guides who accompany mountaineers seeking to conquer Everest's treacherous slopes.

The beauty of the soaring Himalayan peaks, the region's rich cultural heritage, and the fascinating local biodiversity are now part of Sagarmatha National Park. The park, created in 1976, is the world's highest. It covers an area of 443 square miles (1,148 square kilometers) and includes many peaks that rise above 19,685 feet (6,000 meters). They include Lhotse, Cho-Oyu, Nuptse, Amadablam, and Pamori. The United Nations designated the park a World Heritage Site in 1979 for its unique geology, flora and fauna, people and culture, and spectacular landscape.

The Mount Everest (Khumbu) region is the backbone of Nepal's growing tourism industry. Most tourists who come to Nepal do not want to miss an opportunity to see Mount Everest, a once-in-a-lifetime experience. The majority of visitors take a flight from Kathmandu to an airport in the Khumbu region. Others take buses, or even walk part of the way. Mountain flight sightseeing is another option for those who are unable to reach base camp physically. Some, of course, want to climb. Expedition fees in Nepal vary based on the height of the peak. The fee to climb Mount Everest is about $50,000 for a team of up to 5 members, and an additional $10,000 for each additional member (up to a maximum of 10). The fees are smaller for other low-elevation peaks. An additional fee must be deposited for the clearing of garbage by each team; the cost of garbage management for Mount Everest is $4,000 per team, but fees drop to $2,000 for peaks under 26,250 feet (8,000 meters).

Many scaling records and statistics are kept for Mount Everest. Perhaps the darkest is that, for every five people who successfully reach the summit and return, one person dies.

Most records are held by Sherpas, including the first ascent, the fastest climb, and the longest time spent standing naked on the summit (three minutes in subzero temperatures!). In 1963, Jim Whittaker became the first American to reach Everest's summit. Moments later, the late Barry Bishop, an American geographer who worked for the National Geographic Society, followed Whittaker to the top. The mountain has been climbed by an American with an artificial leg (Thomas Whittaker) and another who was blind (Erik Weihenmayer). In 2005, two Nepalese—Ms. Moni Mulepati and Mr. Pem Dorjee—were even married on top of the mountain!

Another attraction of the Everest region is the Everest Marathon, which is listed in the *Guinness Book of World Records* as the marathon conducted at the highest elevation. The Everest Marathon begins at Gorak Shep (17,000 feet; 5,184 meters) and finishes at Namche Bazaar (11,300 feet; 3,446 meters). This amazing footrace began in 1987. By late 2007, it had been conducted 12 times over the rugged course that covers mostly downhill mountain trails. The grand success of the Everest Marathon inspired other such races in the region, including the Tenzing-Hillary Everest Marathon.

Kanchenjunga Region–Mount Kanchenjunga

Mount Kanchenjunga—the "Five Treasures of the Eternal Snows"—takes its name from its five distinct peaks, which are located at the eastern edge of Nepal and extend into neighboring Sikkim. The peaks are believed to represent a repository for the five holy items essential for life: gems, grain, salt, weapons, and holy books. Rising to 28,169 feet (8,586 meters), the mountain is the second highest in Nepal and the third highest in the world. It was first climbed in 1955, two years after Mount Everest was initially scaled. Local people consider the peaks of Kanchenjunga to be the holy place of a patron deity who protects them from possible harm. Kanchenjunga is one of the most famous trekking regions in Nepal for mountain

The red panda is a distant cousin of the larger, and more famous, black-and-white variety usually found in China. This type of panda thrives in the Nepalese region of Kanchenjunga, where it has been seen sleeping in trees with its ringed tail wrapped around itself for warmth. Classified by the World Wildlife Federation as an endangered species, the red panda is threatened by the deforestation of its habitat.

adventurers and climbers. Hiking to the Kanchenjunga area was opened in 1988, making it possible to visit wonderful and unexplored tracts in the eastern Nepalese Himalayas. The absence of roads requires visitors to hike. Their efforts are richly rewarded, however, by the area's beautiful scenery.

The Kanchenjunga area is rich in biodiversity. In 1998, the Kanchenjunga Conservation Area Project (KCAP) was launched by Nepal's government and the World Wildlife Fund (WWF) to conserve the area's flora and fauna. The project has focused attention on encouraging local people to manage their natural resources and improve their livelihood opportunities. The KCAP includes more than 2,000 species of plants. It is also home to 252 species of birds, 22 kinds of mammals, 82 types of insects, 5 varieties of fish, and 6 species of amphibians.

Annapurna Region—Mount Annapurna

Annapurna, the "Goddess of the Harvests," rises to an elevation of 26,545 feet (8,091meters). Lying in the central part of the country, the Annapurna region is another very popular trekking route known as the "classic trek." This region provides a superb panorama of the Himalayas, including the Annapurna and Dhaulagiri ranges. Furthermore, the region offers a vast variety of landscapes and diverse ecological zones. Along the classic trek, one encounters such features as the subtropical Pokhara Valley, extensively terraced hillsides, alpine forest, and even a semidesert near the Tibetan border. The east–west trending ranges are situated just to the north of Pokhara. They include Annapurna, Annapurna II (26,000 feet; 7,925 meters), Annapurna III (24,787 feet; 7,555 meters), and others. Above all, Machhapuchhre (22,943 feet; 6,993 meters) gives an astonishing and unsurpassed panorama to all visitors. The shining peak of Machhapuchhre has never been climbed, out of respect for the belief that it is a holy and sacred place to the local people.

The Annapurna Conservation Area Project (ACAP), established in 1986, is the first and largest conservation project in Nepal. It encompasses the entire Annapurna range, an area of 2,946 square miles (7,629 square kilometers). The ACAP also has involved local people in the conservation and management of the protected area. The region is recognized as a natural paradise and is rich in biodiversity. As a result, it is the primary destination of more than 60 percent of all foreign hikers visiting Nepal. The ACAP collects fees from visitors and uses the funds for biodiversity conservation and environmental protection. The project is home to more than 1,200 plant species, 100 mammals, 478 types of birds, 39 reptiles, 22 amphibians, and many types of butterflies.

The Elusive Yeti

The Himalayas are home to the legendary Yeti—or "Abominable Snowman." This gigantic, yet incredibly elusive "ape man" is a shaggy beast that is reported to roam the high, snow-covered mountains. The name *Yeti* means "rock-living animal." Many folktales exist among the Sherpas, who have believed in the Yeti's existence for many centuries. In traditional Nepalese art, there are a number of paintings of the Yeti as a humanlike creature. According to Sherpas, in 1974, a Yeti attacked a girl who was grazing yaks. Nearby villagers reportedly found several dead yaks with broken necks. Following this event, the villagers were even more convinced of the Yeti's existence.

There is, however, no conclusive evidence to prove that anyone has ever seen or photographed a Yeti—and no other evidence has ever been found to prove their existence. There are occasional reports of a sighting, even by famous mountaineers. Some claim to have seen a dark, humanlike figure in the distance. Others claim to have found strange footprints in the snow, heard a weird sound, or found hair or some other sign of the creature's existence. Who knows? Perhaps future expeditions will stumble upon conclusive evidence of the Yeti's existence. Until then, however, the Abominable Snowman will remain a shadowy and elusive legend of the remote Himalayas.

WEATHER AND CLIMATE

Nepal's conditions of weather (day-to-day atmospheric conditions) and climate (long-term average of the weather) are the result of two primary controls: elevation and the seasonal change in moisture resulting from the South Asian monsoon. On average, temperatures drop about 3.5°F with each 1,000-foot increase in elevation (6.5°C/1,000 meters). For example, if the temperature on a summer afternoon in Kathmandu were 80°F, it would be about 35 degrees colder atop a mountain rising 10,000 feet above the city. Weather conditions and the resulting climatic zones therefore correspond to Nepal's land regions. Narrow east–west trending bands of climate change abruptly within very short north–south distances. In fact, within fewer than 100 miles, one can travel from steaming tropical conditions to sparkling snowfields and glaciers.

As is the case throughout the United States and Canada, Nepal enjoys four distinct seasons—spring, summer, autumn, and winter. Inasmuch as the country is in the Northern Hemisphere, the seasons occur during the same months as they do in North America. In general, spring and autumn are the most pleasant seasons.

The low-lying Terai enjoys a mild, subtropical climate. In the lowlands, summers can be hot and steamy, with temperature and humidity similar to those of the southeastern United States. Temperatures have risen as high as a sweltering 116°F (46.4°C) in the lowland region. Northward, the hill region has a moderate climate. The Kathmandu Valley, at an elevation of 4,500 feet (1,370 meters), experiences a mild climate that ranges from 70°–100°F (20°–30°C) during the summer, and from 30°–64°F (1°–20°C) in the winter. In the mountains, conditions are frigid year-round, dropping to well below zero at high elevations. Mountain valleys, many of which are inhabited, are somewhat warmer; temperature extremes depend on their elevation.

The second primary control of Nepal's atmospheric conditions is the monsoon that affects much of Asia. Fundamentally, the monsoon (which means "season") is a seasonal shift in the wind that is accompanied by a marked change in precipitation. During the late fall, winter, and early spring, the wind blows mainly from the north. Because it comes from the interior of Asia, it is very dry. Little precipitation occurs during this time of year. Toward the end of June, however, the wind changes, blowing from the south off of the tropical waters of the Indian Ocean. Between late June and mid-September, Nepal receives about 90 percent of its annual precipitation. Much of the rain falls as torrential showers that can cause local flooding, mud-flows, and landslides. Because of the almost constant summer cloud cover, temperatures are somewhat milder than during the drier spring and early autumn.

WATER RESOURCES

Nepal is rich in water resources. Many streams begin in Tibet and flow southward into Nepal, where they join tributaries that begin in the country's own snowcapped Himalayas. All streams eventually join the mighty Ganges (Ganga) River in India. Major drainage systems, from west to east across the country, include the Karnali, Gandaki, and Kosi rivers. The western part of Nepal is drained by the Karnali river system. Major tributaries include the Bheri and Seti rivers.

The Gandaki River, which flows through central Nepal (also called the Narayani in Nepal and the Gandak in India) is one of the country's major streams. It, too, has a number of tributaries. The river has been harnessed to produce hydro-electric energy and also is an important source of water for irrigation. It has scoured one of the world's deepest canyons, the Kali Gandaki Gorge (also called Andha Galchi). The Gandaki flowed across the area before the Himalayas began to form. As the mountains gradually rose, the river was able to cut its way downward through the rock. In this way, over a period of millions of years, it was able to create the spectacular canyon. (The same physical process is responsible for Arizona's Grand Canyon of the Colorado River. As the Colorado Plateau gradually rose over a period of millions of years, the river cut through the rock to form the canyon.) The Kosi river system drains the eastern part of Nepal; its main tributary is the Arun.

Nepal's rivers are very fast flowing. Within fewer than 100 miles (160 kilometers), they cascade down thousands of feet of steep terrain. This presents several economic opportunities. First, few countries in the world have greater potential to develop hydroelectric resources. Today, about 80 percent of Nepal's electricity comes from hydro sources, but only 2 percent of the country's hydroelectric potential is harnessed. Future development of this resource, including the sale of energy to India, could give Nepal's economy a much-needed boost. Second, Nepal has become a destination for rafting. This is particularly true for those visitors who seek world-class whitewater streams. Finally, the country's rivers offer spectacular scenery that could become a major tourist attraction.

NATURAL HAZARDS

Nepal is subject to a number of natural hazards. Severe thunderstorms that occur during the summer monsoon season can cause flooding, mudflows, and landslides. At the opposite extreme, a weak monsoon can cause severe drought and famine. In the mountains, snow avalanches pose a threat in inhabited areas. A wall of snow can cascade down a mountain slope with the speed of a race car and sweep away or bury everything in its path.

Earthquakes, although infrequent, pose a major threat to life and property in Nepal. The country lies astride an active seismic zone, created by the clashing of the Indo-Australian and Eurasian plates. The collision created the Himalaya Mountains and movement continues to occur at a rate of about one-third of an inch (0.8 centimeter) each year. Nepal's last major earthquake occurred in 1934; as many as 20,000 people lost their lives directly or indirectly as a result of this devastating event, and up to a quarter of the country's homes were destroyed. Most deaths occurred when people's homes collapsed on them during the tremor. Historically, Nepal experiences a severe earthquake approximately every 75 years. Therefore, another major event is due at any time. With a population that has more than doubled since 1934, and with no changes in building construction, the next earthquake may be much more devastating than those of the past.

The perilous terrain of Nepal leaves many of its citizens vulnerable to natural disasters such as landslides, floods, and mudflows. While monsoon season can signal a good upcoming harvest, there have been times when the rains have triggered massive floods and mudslides, forcing people to be evacuated from their homes.

3

Nepal
Through Time

A ccording to Hindu mythology, Nepalese civilization traces its roots to the "Age of Truth." As legend has it, Manu, the world's first human being and king of the world, is believed to have ruled Nepal during this time. The territory over which he ruled was known as the Land of Truth. It was a place that became famous for spirituality, meditation, and penance during the Silver Age. During the Copper Age, Nepal was a popular place for seekers of eternal freedom and salvation. Today, this territory is known as Nepal. The present time is referred to as the Iron Age, a period highlighted by developments in science and technology. Neolithic tools found in the Kathmandu Valley prove that humans have existed here since before 9,000 B.C. It is possible, of course, that humans have occupied the region for a much longer period of time. Other than as a point of interest, the antiquity of humans in Nepal has little geographical significance.

ANCIENT TIMES

The Nagas are considered the first known people to settle in and around the Kathmandu Valley. According to legend, their king, Banashur, was defeated by Lord Krishna, who established the Gopala Dynasty. The Gopala were cattle herders who are believed to have introduced agricultural activities, including animal husbandry, in the Kathmandu Valley. Bhuktaman (first) and Yakshya Gupta (last) were the popular kings of this dynasty. Another group—the Ahiras—lived in this region. The Ahiras were buffalo herders (Asian buffalo, not to be confused with the American bison). Many historians believe that they defeated the Gopala's king, Yakshya Gupta, after which they ruled for about 200 years.

The Kirat ruled for approximately 1,225 years, from the eighth century B.C. to about A.D. 300. The powerful tribe came to Nepal from the Tibeto-Burman ethnic region of the eastern Himalayas. Several Hindu religious books have described the Kirat Dynasty and their people; they were known to be fierce fighters who were experts at guerrilla warfare. Yalamber, the first king of the Kirat Dynasty, rose to power by defeating the Ahiras Dynasty.

Aryans, who had migrated northward into Nepal from India, ruled the country from about A.D. 300 to 1200. The Licchavi Aryans became one of the most renowned dynasties in ancient Nepalese history. The first Licchavi king, Susupta, came into power by defeating the Kirat king, Gasti. These Aryans ruled the region until perhaps the eighth century. They are recognized for their elitism, prosperity, and the flourishing of culture during their era of control. Advancements were made in language and writing, and they introduced many social reforms. The last record—inscribed in Sanskrit—of the Licchavi Dynasty is dated A.D. 733. According to some historians, however, they continued to hold power until around 1200.

Agriculture was the basis of the economy during this era. The Licchavi kings, however, established both political and business ties with kingdoms to the north and south of Nepal. Business links were strengthened and flourished with the spread of Buddhism and religious pilgrimages. The Shakyas were a group that took their name from a region in the foothills of the Himalayas. Their distinguished dynasty flourished in the Kapilbastu district of Nepal. Gautama Buddha, a son of King Suddhodhana, was the prince of the Shakya Dynasty. Following the death of Gautama Buddha, the dynasty was threatened by Bidhhusak, the king of Kosal, India. As a result, the Shakyas fled to the northern hill part of Nepal and Kathmandu Valley. This region lay among the foothills of the Himalayas, in the farthest northern regions of the Indo-gigantic plains in Nepal.

MEDIEVAL NEPAL (750–1768)

The medieval period of Nepal is poorly documented. Few manuscripts or inscriptions exist that provide a glimpse of the people or of the time. Most available artifacts and manuscripts are of a religious nature. From them, we know that it was a period of little territorial and administrative expansion. It also saw the gradual decline of the Licchavi Dynasty.

Evidently, the period experienced the emergence of a new power, the Newars, who became established by 879. One thing that is known about the period is that it witnessed a profound change in religious practices, with a shift from Buddhism to Hinduism. With the downfall of the Lichhavis, the Malla Dynasty came to power—a position it held from about 1200 to 1769. The Malla came to the Kathmandu Valley from the Malla Kingdom of Gorakhpur in northern India. Under the Malla, the valley rose in importance as a regional center of economy and politics. It continued to benefit from a variety of social, cultural, and economic reforms. The Nepali calendar, Bikram Sambat

Known for their skilled craftsmanship, the Newars ruled Nepal for two dynasties. The reign of Newar rulers left their mark on Nepal, as Hinduism grew and a new calendar was established, along with a caste system. Here, members of a Newar band carry traditional metal pots and beat drums to celebrate the Newari new year 1128, in Kathmandu, on November 10, 2007.

(B.S.), was developed during this period, but with a beginning date 57 years earlier than the Christian calendar (57 B.C. on the Western calendar). However, the period suffered from several raids by Mughal empires located to the south, in India. The worst blow occurred in 1345–1346. A raid under the direction of Sultan Shamsud-din Ilyas of Bengal devastated all major religious shrines and resulted in the widespread looting of properties and jewels.

Jayasthiti Malla, a popular king of the Malla period, unified the major principalities in the valley by 1374. Furthermore, he contributed greatly to the shaping of Nepalese culture, including its society, religion, and political administration. So influential were his deeds that today's Nepalese continue to follow many of the practices he introduced. He is credited with having established Nepal's first complete codification of law. It was based on dharma, the "right way to live" or "proper conduct" concept that is the foundation of several South Asian faiths. Jayasthiti Malla also is credited with having introduced the caste system into Nepal. After 1482, Nepalese history took several sharp turns. Sons of the last Malla ruler, Yakshya Malla, divided the valley into three separate kingdoms and ruled separately.

During the medieval period, people of the Khasa *jati* (tribe) had settled in the western part of Nepal. They migrated from central Asia and settled in the Karnali region. Later, under the leadership of Nagaraj, they established the Khasa Kingdom there. Nagaraj rapidly expanded his territory. The Khasa also made many contributions to Nepal's history and culture. Perhaps the greatest was their language, which served as the parent tongue for the present-day Nepali language.

MODERN NEPAL EMERGES (1742–1816)

By 1559, the Gorkha Kingdom was established in western Nepal by Dravya Shah. This new kingdom further enforced the unification of small principalities. The Shah kings were descendents of a noble family of the Chandrabansi Rajput Dynasty of Chitor, India, who had migrated to Nepal during the fifteenth century. Dravya Shah became king of a Magar (ethnic group)-dominated kingdom by winning a marathon. Later, King Ram Shah (1606–1633) continued expanding the Gorkha state by making allies of various quarrelling kingdoms of the Kathmandu Valley. He introduced several noteworthy reforms, and people still remember him for the saying, "Go to Gorkha (if you are deprived of justice)." Ram Shah's major reforms included abolishment of witchcraft customs and the death penalty. He also introduced new measurement standards for distance and weight, as well as irrigation technology to many remote villages.

Following the death of Narabhupal Shah in 1742, his son Prithvi Narayan Shah became king of the Gorkha Kingdom. He was the first great figure in the history of "modern" Nepal.

Prithvi Narayan Shah used supreme power wisely, and he launched an ambitious program to unify many small and often quarrelsome kingdoms. At an early age, he visited Kathmandu, the Makawanpur District, and northern India. His visit to India helped him realize the possible danger of a northward expansion into Nepal by Britain's Indian Empire. Seeking to strengthen his own hand, he set out to conquer the Kathmandu Valley and merge the region into a single kingdom.

Prithvi Narayan Shah visited Varanasi (a holy city on the Ganges River) to purchase modern weapons. While in India, he also examined the condition of states in northern India and the activities of the British East India Company. In Nepal, he established a number of military barracks, increased troop numbers and strength, and trained them in the use of modern weapons. Finally, he was ready to implement his plan to expand the Gorkha Kingdom.

Initially, he attempted to develop an alliance with neighboring states. If that failed, he went to war against them. The Gorkhas applied a blockade strategy, in which they closed all trade routes into a state. Thus cut off, their enemies were left with little choice: starve or surrender. After a six-month blockade, Gorkha troops finally captured Kirtipur, a city located about six miles from Kathmandu, in 1767. This set the stage for the dramatic capture of Kathmandu. Prithvi Narayan Shah and his troops invaded the city while people were celebrating a religious festival, and they were able to capture it without loss of life. In fact, after being crowned as the king of Kathmandu, Prithvi Narayan Shah continued the festival in 1768. The previous king of Kathmandu, Jayaprakash Malla, fled the region. Soon, the Gorkhas added other kingdoms, such as the Patan and Bhaktapur. Thus, the king of Gorkha became ruler of the entire Kathmandu Valley and beyond. He declared Kathmandu the capital of a greater and increasingly unified Nepal.

Prithvi Narayan Shah's work was not yet finished. He continued his campaign of territorial expansion—his Kathmandu victory was little more than a rehearsal of the Gorkha's military power in the region. By 1773, Gorkha troops controlled several western and almost all eastern Kirat states and had invaded neighboring Sikkim. The Gorkha campaign of territorial expansion suffered a temporary blow when Prithvi Narayan Shah died in 1775. However, it was not long before Gorkha expansion continued, including the establishment of strategic and diplomatic ties with the Palpa Kingdom. Furthermore, Gorkha troops took control of Almora by 1790 (in India, to the west of Nepal) and Kangara (located still farther to the west and the most distant area ever conquered by Gorkha troops) in 1809.

Historically, Prithvi Narayan Shah is best known for the invaluable guidelines on statesmanship that he put forward for his descendants. His *divyopadesh* (divine counsel) is a set of sayings that remains valuable today. The sayings provide guidance for those involved in crafting foreign policy and addressing national development issues. A very popular saying is that "Nepal is a yam between two stones." Prithvi Narayan Shah realized that Nepal's location between two large and powerful countries—British India and China—placed his land in peril. He advised that balanced and friendly relations between Nepal and its neighbors would be essential if national sovereignty were to be saved.

The death of Prithvi Narayan Shah led to an unfortunate power struggle in the royal court. Palace politics led Nepal to a disastrous situation, in which military power faded, the expansion campaign was halted, and the country's economy was in shambles. Meanwhile, Nepal faced pressure from both China and British India. The latter conflict would result in the greatest shock in Nepalese history.

Nepalese troops invaded Tibet in 1788 and 1791, closed the trade routes, and claimed control of several mountain passes along the border. To further bolster their buffer against China, the Nepalese government signed a trading treaty with British India. Unfortunately (for the Nepalese), Nepal was betrayed by the British. British India did not want to antagonize China, a sleeping giant. In 1792, Nepal was forced to sign a treaty with China to stop Chinese forces that resulted in the loss of territory to, and trading privileges with, Tibet.

To the west, Nepalese troops had claimed territories on the southern plain, including Kumaon, Kangara, and Butwal. However, the southern campaign to acquire these lands had been long and costly for Nepalese troops. Ultimately, a bitter dispute between Nepal and the British East India Company over lands in the Terai erupted into a full-blown war between the two. The conflict raged from 1814 to 1816, but ultimately the Nepalese troops were no match for the British East India Company. They were outmanned and lacked the modern weapons that the British could provide to its East India Company troops. In 1816, Nepal was forced to sign a unilateral treaty with the British East India Company. However, it was a historic—and, in some ways, glorious—war for Nepalese troops. True, Nepal lost part of its territorial claims in the western hills, a few areas to the east, and some of its very productive southern lands. Yet, the treaty increased the British Indian presence (including trade) in Kathmandu, and fierce Nepalese mountain warriors were included in the British Indian force. These Gorkha fighters became famous for their strength and bravery in the British army's brigade of Gorkhas and the Indian army's Gorkha regiments.

RANA REGIME (1846–1950)

Following the events of 1816, Nepal once again descended into political chaos. Eventually, however, an ambitious young man, Jung Bahadur, emerged as a leader. He had joined the army in 1832 at the age of 16. By 1841, he had become a bodyguard for the king, and his influence continued to grow. As an opportunist, Jung Bahadur was lying in wait; his opportunity soon arrived. A meeting between Bahadur and Queen Rajendra Laxmi became violent when the queen's supporters turned against Bahadur. Bahadur, however, slaughtered many of his opponents and emerged victorious. Eventually, he rose to the position of supreme army leader in the royal court. In this role, he immediately took control of the government and exiled more than 6,000 of his perceived enemies to India.

By the mid-nineteenth century, Jung Bahadur had established a hereditary regime that would place Nepal in the grips of a family dictatorship for more than 100 years. As a result of his dictatorial leadership, writers of Nepalese history have not treated him kindly. He remains, however, a well-known figure in his country's past. Jung Bahadur is famous for his bravery, intelligence, command, and many of his deeds, and he took a number of positive and innovative steps toward improving Nepal. For example, he attempted to make government less bureaucratic and the courts more accountable. He also attempted to modernize the country.

Jung Bahadur is also recognized for another important deed—his historic trip to Great Britain from April 1850 to February 1851. This event marked the first time in history that a powerful Nepalese leader had ventured far from his homeland. The tour helped to solidify relations between Nepal and British India and further secured Nepal's sovereignty. He realized that good relations with the British East India Company could help to maintain Nepal's independence. The trip also afforded him a broad view of the outer world, modern developments, industrialization, and the European lifestyle.

In 1854, Jung Bahadur drafted and launched the *Muluki Ain,* a series of administrative procedures and legal frameworks that addressed a variety of issues. With the help of the Muluki Ain, Jung Bahadur took control of all state power.

Jung Bahadur also tried to repair the broken relations with Tibet. In 1856, a treaty was signed that gave Nepal duty-free privileges on trade and permitted a resident (business office) in the Tibetan capital, Lhasa. In 1857, Jung Bahadur personally headed a military campaign that crushed the Sepoy Revolt

Section 3rd   No. 7

SEEPOYS

Indians in military service to European countries were known as sepoys, a rank considered to be equal to private. In May 1857, Indian soldiers were forced to use ammunition cartridges greased in pork and beef fat, violating both their Muslim and Hindu faiths. This led to the Sepoy Revolt of 1857, resulting in the sepoys killing their British superiors in the military, their takeover in Delhi, and their eventual defeat by the British army.

in northern India. His leadership role earned him firm British support for his government. For his effort, Jung Bahadur received the honorary title of *Rana* (a title of martial glory bestowed on Rajput princes in northern India). This honor made him Jung Bahadur Rana, followed by all his descendants. Thereafter, their century-long rein of power was called the "Rana regime." He ruled the country until 1877 and died during a hunting campaign in the Terai.

Following Jung Bahadur Rana's death, Nepalese politics again fell into disarray. There were, however, a few subsequent prime ministers who are recognized positively for their contributions to social, political, or economic reform. One such prime minister was Dev Shamser, who was forced to resign and seek exile in India. His mistake? He introduced progressive reforms such as the release of female slaves, the establishment of schools, and the publication of *Gorkhapatra,* Nepal's first newspaper.

Under Prithvi Narayan Shah, Nepal was unified. He also established that the king had the supreme power to rule the country. Jung Bahadur, on the other hand, snatched complete power from the king. His Muluki Ain codes gave him the power to make any and all political decisions for the country. Thus, the monarchy held little political power, and the position of king or queen was mainly ceremonial for more than a century. There were, however, some important reforms introduced during the Rana regime. They include the abolishment of *Sati Pratha*, the practice of a wife throwing herself onto her dead husband's funeral pyre; the abolishment of slavery in 1920; the establishment of Tri-Chandra College and several high schools; the development of a hydroelectric plant; the creation of the Nepal Industrial Board; and the building of several mills and factories.

During World War I (1914–1918), thousands of Nepalese people served in the military, on the side of the Allies. As a result, in 1923, a Treaty of Perpetual Peace and Friendship was signed between Nepal and the British government, which guaranteed Nepal's independence. This historic event was one of the most important milestones in Nepalese history; it was the first time Nepal had been involved in a conflict far beyond its own border. Of course, it also helped to solidify the Rana dictatorship in Nepal.

POLITICAL PARTIES

After India became independent in 1947, a new wave of political awareness appeared in Nepal and among Nepalese political figures. Newspapers strongly supported a move toward democracy and were very critical of the Rana regime. There were outbreaks of rioting. The government cracked down, resulting in hundreds of people being arrested and imprisoned. Many others fled the country, where they could continue their fight against the Rana dictatorship from a safer haven in India. India's independence obviously had weakened the Rana dictatorship in Nepal. Soon, the exiled Nepalese began to unite. They formed the Nepali National Congress (NNC), a political party that was officially dedicated to the establishment of a democratic government in Nepal. To achieve this, of course, the Rana regime had to be destroyed.

Reacting to the growing crisis in Nepal, Prime Minister Padma Shamser announced some reforms, such as Nepal's first constitution in 1948. Such measures failed to silence critics of the government. Shamser's successor, autocratic Prime Minister Mohan Shamser, banned political parties and suppressed progressive activities in the country. This led to the establishment of the Nepali Congress (NC), a party formed in 1950 by merging the Nepali Democratic Congress and the NNC. The Nepali Congress formally decided to conduct an armed struggle to overthrow the Rana government.

Late in 1950, King Tribhuvan Bir Bikram Shah, who himself was against the Rana regime, took asylum in the Indian embassy in Kathmandu. The Mukti Sena (Liberation Army) of the Nepali Congress began its attack in the Terai, thereby initiating revolution in Nepal. Mohan Shamser found himself in a critical situation, because he had lost much of his Nepalese support; in addition, the Nepalese rebel leaders had strong support from India's leaders. By January 1951, the Mukti Sena controlled much of Nepal, and many of the government troops had surrendered to the rebels.

On January 8, 1951, with assistance from the Indian government, a treaty was negotiated between the Rana family, the king, and the Nepali Congress. King Tribhuvan returned from exile to Kathmandu in February, and a new interim government was formed. It was headed by Mohan Shamser and included five Ranas and five Nepali Congress party members. The coalition government failed, however, for several reasons. The king exercised his power and appointed a new government that did not include any Rana members. The new government was headed by the Nepali Congress leader, Matrika Prasad Koirala. This arrangement placed the Nepalese government under the control of two major power blocs in 1951: the king and the political parties.

In the mid-twentieth century, Nepal faced many problems and challenges. The country was one of the world's most isolated in terms of global linkages and awareness. Modern facilities were concentrated in Kathmandu; elsewhere, conditions were primitive. The country also suffered from a very poor infrastructure. It was difficult for the Nepalese to travel from place to place, or to ship goods. Communications, power, and other amenities that were commonplace in much of the world were largely lacking throughout much of Nepal.

Political turmoil continued. The major target of the interim government was to hold an election for a constituent assembly (Parliament) under an interim constitution. However, the king continued to postpone the assembly election, preferring to wait for a "favorable political environment." Following the death of King Tribhuvan, his son Mahendra Bir Bikram Shah

Despite being elected as prime minister of Nepal in the country's first exercise of democracy, Bishweshor Prasad Koirala was thrown in jail by King Mahendra. Political parties were banned and a new political system was implemented after the monarch took over Nepal. Pictured is King Mahendra and his wife during coronation ceremonies.

took over as ruler in 1955. Finally, in February 1959, an election was held. The Nepali Congress won the majority of seats in the Parliament and formed the government. Bishweshor Prasad Koirala—younger brother of Matrika Prasad Koirala and the popular leader of the NC—headed the government. He was the first elected prime minister of Nepal's modern era.

Unfortunately, the king sacked the NC government in 1961, with the help of the army. The situation turned chaotic as political party members began to protest. The king's response was to ban all political parties and jail most of the party leaders.

PANCHAYAT SYSTEM (1961–1990)

King Mahendra introduced a new constitution and the *panchayat* (party-less political) system in December 1962. The panchayat system claimed to be democratic, at least in Nepal's sociopolitical context. In actuality, the king ensured that he held supreme power over the panchayat system, to which he gave full support. Thus, in reality, it was direct authoritarian rule by the king. Mahendra introduced the National Planning Council, which, in turn, introduced four administrative tiers throughout the country: national, regional, zonal, district, and village panchayat.

Former leader Bishweshor Prasad Koirala was released from jail and traveled to India, where he continued the movement for democracy in his homeland. The panchayat system, meanwhile, did contribute to some progress. Under its direction, priority was given to malaria eradication, highway construction, hydropower development, and expansion of irrigation. It also promoted improvements in banking, foreign relations, industrial growth, and resettlement in the Terai. A land reform program eliminated the large Rana estates. Similarly, Muluki Ain was replaced by a new legal code in 1963.

In 1972, Birendra Bir Bikram Shah Dev ascended to the throne. He was keenly aware of the dismal political situation in his own country, but he also recognized the growing importance of regional and global politics. Therefore, in 1980, he offered a referendum to choose between a multiparty system or a reformed democratic panchayat system. The referendum results were in favor of the panchayat system. Though this was a victory for the king, he quickly reestablished freedom of speech and political activities. Bishweshor Prasad Koirala, who had returned to the country in 1976, advocating reconciliation with the king, also accepted the result.

For a time, it appeared that Nepalese politics were on the right track. The constitution was amended for the third time in 1980. Nepal was ruled by a king-nominated government and Rastriya Panchayat, a Parliament comprising 111 members. Unfortunately, Bishweshor Prasad Koirala died in July 1982; it was a great loss to the Nepalese democratic movement and to the Nepali Congress.

Despite constant political turmoil, some progress occurred in the economy during the panchayat era. Additionally, the king had achieved recognition in international affairs. For example, he earned widespread respect for his proposal to make Nepal a "zone of peace" and a member of the South Asian Association for Regional Cooperation. Unfortunately, the panchayat system received a great shock when India blocked all of the linkages between itself and Nepal once the treaty affecting trade and transportation expired. The blockade disrupted nearly every aspect of life within the country, and it served as a cruel reminder to the Nepalese people of the disadvantages of being landlocked.

The country suffered a critical shortage of imported goods, including petroleum products—for which it depended exclusively upon imports. During the blockade, Nepal's economic growth plummeted from an annual rate of 9.7 percent in 1987–1988 to 1.5 percent a year later. In 1990, the Nepali Congress Party announced a new anti-panchayat movement for the restoration of multiparty democracy. Thus, the people's movement was launched, forming an alliance with the United Left Front parties under the supreme leadership of NC leader Ganeshman Singh.

In response to the renewed call for democracy, a series of spontaneous and turbulent mass demonstrations occurred in major cities throughout the country. People took to the streets, demanding restoration of the multiparty democracy, human

In 1990 an anti-panchayat movement in Nepal sparked mass demonstrations against the monarchy, which led to the reinstatement of a democratic, multiparty system. King Birenda, Mahendra's successor, later declared a prime minister for the Nepalese Parliament, and the first election was held in 1991.

rights, and fundamental freedoms. The grand success of the *bandh* (general strike) in Kathmandu spread rapidly to other cities, resulting in complete stagnation of the country's economy. The people's movement lasted fewer than two months and resulted in the loss of 50 lives and thousands of injuries.

Unable to control widespread public marches, increasing casualties, and eroding support for the monarchy, King Birendra declared a multiparty democracy. This was accomplished by lifting the ban on political parties, which occurred in April 1990. The Rastriya Panchayat was dissolved. The president of the Nepali Congress, Krishna Prasad Bhattarai, formed a cabinet comprising four members from the Nepali Congress, three from the United Left Front, two human rights activists, and two royal nominees. As the goal of the interim government, a new constitution was proclaimed on November 9, 1990. The following May, an election was held for members of a House of Representatives; the Nepali Congress once again won the majority of seats. Girija Prasad Koirala—the youngest brother of Matrika Prasad and Bishweshor Prasad Koirala—served as prime minister.

DEMOCRATIC MULTIPARTY SYSTEM

In 1990, the interim government proclaimed the new democratic constitution, which established fundamental human rights, a parliamentary democracy, and a constitutional monarchy. The Nepali Congress Party won the majority of seats and formed the government in 1991. It was only the second elected democratic government in Nepal's history. Unfortunately, the Parliament was dissolved due to internal conflict within the ruling Nepali Congress Party. The government conducted another general election in November 1994, in which no party gained a majority.

As a result of the stalemate, the Nepal Communist Party, United Marxist and Leninist (UML), formed a minority government for the first time in Nepal. It was headed by Man Mohan

Adhikary and was the world's first Communist monarchy. Political instability continued, with the formation of several unsuccessful coalition governments during the next five years. During this period, a Maoist insurgency gained strength. In 1999, the NC won the majority of seats in Parliament, but it could not establish a stable government. Several short-lived governments, one after another, were headed by Krishna Prasad Bhattarai, Girija Prasad Koirala, and Sher Bahadur Deuba.

Maoists (Communists) began an insurgency in February 1996. Brutal killings, bombings, and torture were widespread, particularly in rural parts of the country. Peace talks were held, to no avail; by 2006, more than 13,000 people had lost their lives. On June 1, 2001, the country was shocked by a massacre of the royal family that remains a mystery to the Nepalese people. Many Nepalese do not believe the "official report" that blamed Crown Prince Dipendra for the slaughter. According to the report, he shot and killed all of his family members, including the king and queen, his brother and sister, and a number of relatives. Soon after, Prince Gyanendra ascended to the throne. In 2002, he suddenly dismissed the elected government, took over all executive power, and dissolved the Parliament. King Gyanendra then nominated several short-lived governments, none of which were able to successfully govern the country. The outer world was shocked when King Gyanendra dismissed the government for a second time. On February 1, 2005, he declared a state of emergency. Many politicians were jailed, and others were placed under house arrest. Freedom of the press was ended. The country's adverse political situation led the mainstream political parties closer to Maoist rebels, who sought to overthrow the monarchy. Ultimately, in November 2005, the various parties signed a 12-point letter of understanding designed to end the political instability.

In April 2006, massive pro-democracy demonstrations took place in Nepal. They were led by mainstream political parties, including the Maoist rebels, and were successful in ending the direct rule of King Gyanendra. Parliament was reinstated and quickly declared Nepal to be a secular nation, over which the king had little power. He no longer served as the head of state, or as commander of the Nepalese army. In November 2006, Nepal's government and the Maoist rebels signed a landmark peace accord that ended the 10-year insurgency.

4

People
and Culture

M odern Nepal, which lies between India and Tibet, presents a complex diversity of people, languages, and ethnic
groups. Visitors observe Nepalese people—their societies,
appearances, and cultures—as a complex combination resulting from
centuries of multiethnic and multilingual interactions. Broadly, three
major geographical regions reflect three different ethnic communities and language groups. Such diverse communities and languages
have resulted in a complex pattern of customs and beliefs that make
it hard to generalize about Nepalese society, its people, and its culture
in general.

POPULATION
Despite its small territory, rural poverty, and subsistence economy,
Nepal's population is home to approximately 29 million people. This

gives the country a population density of nearly 410 people per square mile (158 per square kilometer). Yet, that figure tells only part of the story. In the fertile, low-lying Terai region and Kathmandu Valley, several thousand people can be crammed into each square mile of area. In fact, population pressure is a huge problem in the Terai belt, which is home to more than half of all Nepalese. About 70 percent of the land, however, is owned by landlords, who receive much of the area's agricultural production in the form of rent. As a result, landlessness is widespread and creates a huge socioeconomic problem in the country. In the mountains, on the other hand, hundreds of square miles may be home to no one. In 2007, the population was growing at an annual rate of about 2.1 percent, a full percent higher than the world's average rate of increase.

Much of the demographic (statistical) data clearly point to Nepal's status as a less-developed country (LDC). Nearly 84 percent of its people, for example, live in the countryside, where they are dependent upon subsistence agriculture for their survival. Only about 16 percent of all Nepalese are urban, and most of those live in Kathmandu, which is home to more than one million people. By comparison, worldwide, rural and urban populations are almost equally divided; in the developed world, about 75 percent of the population is urban. Slightly more than half (54 percent) of the Nepalese population is literate—able to read and write—which is very low by world standards. Additionally, life expectancy at birth is a relatively short 60.56 years—again, very low by world standards. Clearly, Nepal has a long way to go in improving the quality of life for its people.

Statistics show that more than 30 percent of the population is living below the poverty line. As a result, thousands of young people have emigrated to India and various countries in Southeast Asia and the Middle East in search of employment. During the past decade, the country has experienced an unusually high rate of internal population displacement and

Because of Nepal's heavy reliance on rice, the Nepalese government has declared a day during the monsoon season "National Paddy Day." Considered to be the most auspicious day for paddy farming, holiday activities include cultivating paddy seedlings *(above)* and traditional cultural performances.

out-migration. This is one of the many negative results of the Maoist insurgency and resulting terrorism. On the other hand, the country has received a large influx (more than 100,000) of Bhutanese refugees since 1990. There also are a number of Tibetan refugees in the country.

LIFESTYLE

Keeping in mind the fact that Nepal is about the size of Alabama, the reader may be shocked to learn that more than 40 different ethnic groups speak a total of about 70 different languages. Few comparable areas of the world can match this diversity. Culture in general—and the caste system in particular—may give the first-time visitor to Nepal a cultural shock. Each family and each individual accepts and lives by the caste-imposed codes of conduct and status. With more than 80 percent of the country's population being rural, most Nepalese abide by traditional cultural customs and values. In the cities, however, young people in particular have been influenced by Western popular culture. They are less apt to rigidly follow the guidelines of caste.

The foundation of Nepalese society is the extended family. Most families live together, with three generations—from grandparents to grandchildren—sharing a home. Traditionally, marriages (including the selection of mates) were arranged by parents. Today, such customs are more relaxed, having given way (particularly in cities) to what is known as *modern arranged marriages.* In this system, young males and females meet, fall in love, decide to marry, and then let their parents arrange the union. The traditional arranged marriage system still prevails, however, in most rural areas. Family ties involving both sides of the newly formed family union are much closer than in the United States. They are considered to be a very important form of social capital during difficult times. Marriage ceremonies are performed on a date determined by an astrologer or priest. The ceremony can take from a few hours to three days; the duration depends on the families' caste and socioeconomic class. It may be conducted at the bride's home, or in any religious spot, such as a temple. The legal age for marriage is 19 years for girls and 21 years for boys.

High importance is placed on sons within family and society. Sons are responsible for taking care of elderly parents and making their lives easier after retirement. It is believed that some religious rites, such as funeral processions, should be performed by a son. This is thought to pave the way for a peaceful entry to heaven and the next life.

Nepalese people possess a number of characteristic traits. Most, for example, are honest and straightforward. They tend to be devout in their faith, yet they are respectful of others' beliefs. Nepal has not suffered the religious intolerance experienced in so many other countries. The people also tend to be remarkably flexible and pragmatic. In general, they are recognized for their patience, good humor, a quick smile, and being slow to anger.

Despite these traits, Nepalese have earned a worldwide reputation as fierce fighters. Many Nepalese arts and crafts provide a revealing glimpse of religious life among Hindus, Buddhists, and people of other cultural communities.

A DIVERSE PEOPLE

Nepal's human diversity can best be studied regionally. Simply stated, people who remain geographically separated from one another tend to retain their individuality. Mountains, valleys, and the close proximity of other lands and peoples (e.g., China, Tibet, and India) contribute to regional variations. Rural people living traditional lifestyles, in particular, tend to retain their folk customs and practices. In addition to isolation, marriage between individuals of different castes is prohibited. This practice reinforces group differences, even within particular ethnic groups. Kathmandu represents the best example of interaction among diverse ethnic groups from all parts of the country.

The Mountain (Himalayan) Region

The people and culture—including language, religion, and lifestyle—of the northern mountain (Himalaya) region are highly influenced by Tibetan origin and values. Most people are migrants from Bhot (Tibet) and practice the Buddhist faith. The major ethnic groups of the mountain region are the Thakalis, Tamangs, and Sherpas.

Thakalis live along the Kaligandaki Valley in central Nepal. They were once famous salt traders between India and Tibet. Today, many of them run tourist hotels along the Jomsom and Annapurna trek routes, and in the city of Pokhara. They originally were Buddhist, but today some follow Hinduism.

The word *Tamangs* literally means "horse soldier." These people live in the northern hills of the Kathmandu Valley, and Tibetan culture has a strong influence in their daily life. Tamangs are hard workers and very sober in their nature. Traditionally, most of them worked on farms. Recently, however,

Located on the way to the base camp of Mount Everest, Tengboche Monastery is visited by over 30,000 people a year. Destroyed once by an earthquake and again by a fire, rebuilding the monastery has become very important to the Nepalese and Sherpa communities because of its cultural significance.

many of them have become involved in making Tibetan souvenirs, carpets, and *thanka* (banner-like paintings), which are very popular among tourists in Nepal.

Sherpas are the world-famous ethnic group that lives in the Khumbu (Everest) region of the Himalayas. They migrated to Nepal from the Kham of Tibet in the late 1400s. Sherpas follow and celebrate Tibetan Buddhism. Monasteries such as

Tengboche are the common gathering place where local Sherpas celebrate festivals, such as Dumje and Mani Rimdu. Their traditional economy focused upon farming and livestock herding, as well as some trade. Since the 1950s, however, they have become extensively involved in mountaineering expeditions and other aspects of the regional tourist industry.

The Hill Region

The hill region's mild climate makes it the most comfortable place to live in Nepal. The south-facing slopes and lower valley floor, in particular, are extensively farmed and support an easy lifestyle. Distinct ethnic minorities still can be found in different parts of the hill region, including the Kirati, Newar, Gurungs, Magars, Brahmin, and Chhettri.

The Kiratis are of Tibeto-Burmese descent and are distinctive because of their Mongoloid physical features. Though their traditional religion is considered to be different, they still worship Lord Shiva and follow Hinduism. Kiratis, who ruled Nepal in about the seventh century, migrated to the eastern hill region from the Kathmandu Valley. Kiratis are well-known Himalayan warriors; they are the world-renowned soldiers who filled the British Gorkha regiments. The curve-bladed *khukuri*, or "Gorkha knife," is the most important Gorkha weapon. Although it has less value in today's world of automatic weapons and nuclear power, the Nepalese and Gorkha armies keep it as a symbol of bravery. The khukuri also is an important element of Nepalese national dress.

Newars occupy the Kathmandu Valley and are descendants of its original rulers. Their origin and history remain a mystery, although physically they appear to be a blend of Kiratis and Caucasians. The Newari language is very complex and difficult to learn, and it is distinct from any other languages spoken in the country. Furthermore, Newari culture is quite complex and distinctive. It includes a number of customs not found elsewhere in the country, such as *kumari,* a young girl who is worshiped as a living goddess. Newars, like other ethnic groups in Nepal, can be identified by their traditional dress. Today, they are known as farmers, excellent artisans, and shrewd businesspersons.

Gurungs are the dominant ethnic group of the central midlands and southern slope of the Annapurna region. They are of Tibeto-Burmese origin and migrated into Nepal from western Tibet. Attractive Ghandruk is the largest Gurung settlement. The picturesque community of about 11,000 people offers a stunning view of the Machhapuchhre and Annapurna range. Many Gurungs also became famous as members of the British Gorkha regiment. The Gurungs have a tradition called *Rodi,* a club environment in which boys and girls sing, dance, and socialize with one another.

The Magar ethnic group dominates the midlands zone of central and western Nepal. They, too, came from the north and are of Tibeto-Burmese origin. Magars are also brilliant fighters. Most of the Magar people are involved in agricultural activities. Although they have their own distinct language, dress, and customs, they are increasingly influenced by Hinduism.

Brahmins and Chhettris are the most dominant upper-caste tribes and are scattered throughout the country. However, they are most heavily concentrated in the middle hill region and the far west. They account for about 30 percent of the country's total population. Religiously and socially, Brahmins are respected for their purification and knowledge of ritual performances as priests. Brahmins are generally vegetarians who abstain from alcohol. Chhettris are mostly warriors and rulers. Most people of these castes also work in farms and have a very simple life. Yet, Brahmins maintain a distinct and prestigious status throughout the country. The caste system has been abolished for decades, but it is still deeply rooted in Nepalese society. People of lower castes are highly marginalized, both socially and economically.

The Terai Region

The Terai region is known as Madhesh, and the people of Terai origin are called Madheshi. They are now the major inhabitants of the Terai, though the Nepalese Terai used to be densely forested. It was very sparsely settled because of the high incidence of malaria. After malaria was eradicated in the 1950s, the region began to be settled—first quite slowly, but then as a flood of humanity. A government resettlement program worked as a catalyst to bring thousands of hill and mountain people into the Terai. Today, the Terai has become an agglomeration of ethnic groups representing people from throughout the country.

Tharus are believed to be the earliest inhabitants of the Terai region. They are more concentrated in the far western part of the lowland. Most Tharus have Tibeto-Burmese physical characteristics, but their origin is blurred. Today, most of them are Hindus. For many generations, the Tharus were exploited as bonded laborers by local landlords. In 2000, the government freed all the *Kamaiyas* (bonded laborers); nonetheless, many problems relating to land and living have not yet been resolved.

The Maithili population is concentrated in the central to eastern Terai region. In the distant past, they were the people of the Mithila Kingdom, which stretched across the present-day border into India. Maithili people follow Hinduism and have their own rich and ancient culture. Their language is similar in some ways to Hindi and Urdu. Maithili painting is very popular in Nepal and northern India.

THE CASTE SYSTEM

Caste—into which a person is born—and status are dominant cultural features in Nepalese society. Each of them contributes to a sharply defined hierarchical social system and the resulting respect an individual receives from others. Caste determines a person's place in society, including profession, marriage, and personal interaction in the community and even within the

The caste system creates a hierarchical society, where people are born into certain classes that determine their line of work and status in life. In 2001, the Nepalese government outlawed discrimination against the people of lower castes, allowing those people to use village water pumps *(above)*, pray in Hindu temples, and for their children to receive an equal education.

family. The caste system is a trait of Hindu culture and society. In today's modern society, it poses a growing stumbling block to widespread acceptance of the Hindu faith and its practices.

The caste system was implemented in ancient times as a way of dividing people by work and occupation. Wise and knowledgeable people were graded as Brahmins and assigned to teach and counsel people in the society. The bravest people were selected as Chhettris and assigned to protect people in the society. Some strong people were grouped as Baishyas and assigned the duty of supplying goods in the role of business-men. The last group were Sudras, people who were assigned to work in the fields and other primary industries, such as logging and mining. According to Hindu mythology, the God Brahma is the creator of Earth and its creatures. Thus, each caste is a product of part of Brahma's body. The Brahmins, for example, were created from the mouth of Brahma; Chhettris were from his arms; Baishyas were born from his lap; and Sudras were cre-ated from the feet, symbolizing the bearing of weight.

In the traditional classification system, the four-caste hier-archy further includes 36 *Varnas* (social categories). Regard-ing the caste system, King Prithvi Narayan Shah symbolically referred to Nepal as "A Garden of Four Jats and Thirty-six Var-nas." Today, in a very general sense, Nepalese society is divided into three major caste groups. They are: *Tagadhari* (wearers of the holy sacred cord), which includes Brahmin, Chhettri, and Thakuri; *Matvali* (liquor drinking), which includes ethnic groups such as the Gurung, Rai, and Limbu; and *Pani Nachalne* (untouchables), which includes the various occupational castes. This caste system was first codified by the ruler Jung Bahadur Rana as the National Legal Code (Muluki Ain) of 1854.

LANGUAGE

Few countries in the world of comparable size share Nepal's diversity of languages. Some 70 different tongues are spoken by the Nepalese people. Nepali is the dominant language, but it is the mother tongue for about half (47.8 percent) of the population. Many of the other tongues are the native languages of various minority ethnic groups. They include: Maithali (12.3 percent), Bhojpuri (7.4 percent), Tharu (5.8 percent), Tamang (5.1 percent), Newari (3.6 percent), Magar (3.3 percent), and Awadhi (2.4 percent). Most well-educated people, and those involved in government or business, also speak English.

RELIGION

Religion is very important to most Nepalese. The influence of religion is evident in the everyday life of people throughout the country. Brahmins, for example, are socially and religiously obliged to perform basic rituals relating to cleanliness, meditation, and worship (*puja*) at home every day. Such activities are also followed by many members of other castes at home. Most people also worship in a nearby temple each day.

Kathmandu is widely recognized as being a "City of Temples," or "City of Gods." Nearly every house has a religious symbol on or by the front door or in the yard. People also perform occasional worship at home. This activity can last between 1 to 10 days, but it may continue for months if formally organized by a community. Puja recognizes that God is not far from each of us. Nepalese people worship through prayer and ritual. They believe that God is everywhere around them. Therefore, people believe that God can influence humans' everyday lives in numerous ways.

In general, puja refers to the prayer and worship of the gods and goddesses and the offering of different foods, fruits, and other things. People also offer *Namaste* to greet the divinity. This is done by raising and joining both hands, with palms close to one's heart, and bowing the head frontward. Namaste signifies a "reverential salutation to the inner divine," and it means, "I honor the divine inside of you."

Hinduism

Hinduism is the world's oldest religion, dating back to about 1500 B.C. It is also the world's third-largest religion; about 13 percent of the world's population follows the faith, most of whom live in India, Sri Lanka, and Nepal. At the root of Hinduism is the recognition of a trinity of gods: *Brahma* (the creator), *Vishnu* (the preserver), and *Shiva* (the destroyer). Additionally, there are many forms and avatars (incarnations, or the presence of a spirit in earthly form) of gods and goddesses. *Vedas* are the sacred and holy scriptures of the Hindu faith. Although it is not known when they were written, it is believed that the Vedas are the most ancient texts in the world. The primary sacred texts include four Vedas. Other Hindu holy books are the *Ramayana* and the *Mahabharat*. *Bhagavad-Gita* is the main sacred book of the Hindus. It is a poem that describes a conversation between Lord Krishna and the warrior Arjun in the battlefield. Lord Krishna is believed to be the eighth incarnation of Lord Vishnu.

Have you ever wondered why Hindus hold life sacred, including cows? It is because they believe in reincarnation, or the rebirth of a soul in a new body after death. In other words, they believe in a cycle of birth, life, death, and rebirth through an infinite series of lives here on Earth. This life cycle is called *Sansara*, and it is determined by *Karma*. Karma is the lifetime sum total of one's deeds—both good and bad. It is Karma that determines the fate of an individual's soul in the next life. A good life, full of good deeds and devotion, assures one of a rebirth of high status. A life of bad deeds, however, can cause one to be reborn as a lower life form. Because all life forms are believed to be incarnate souls (possibly even a deceased relative), life, itself, is held sacred.

In this way, Hindus view everyday suffering and happiness, poverty and wealth, scorn and prestige, and other traits as the natural consequence of deeds from a previous lifetime. Such beliefs and practices have resulted in a fatalistic way of thinking among Hindus that greatly influences their everyday lives and actions.

The caste system is associated primarily with the Hindu religion. As previously noted, this rigid system defines one's rights by birth. One is born into one's caste. Caste determines each person's *dharma* (way of living), including his or her behavior, duties, and expectations. It further prescribes one's social, economic, religious, and political position, as well as the way one interacts with members of other castes. Caste status cannot be changed; it remains throughout one's lifetime. However, violation of one's obligations can cause descendants to be born into a lower caste. Today, the caste system—which was outlawed more than a half century ago—is beginning to change. Particularly in cities, people's beliefs and actions are increasingly influenced by education, modernity, and Western culture.

Constitutionally, Nepal was the world's only Hindu Kingdom until 2006. The king of Nepal was said to be an avatar of Lord Vishnu and the patron (protector) of the Hindu faith worldwide. In May 2006, however, the Nepalese Parliament voted to turn Nepal into a secular country, thereby ending the special Hindu Kingdom status. The difficult decision was one of several that the government made to coax the Maoist rebels to peacefully join the political process.

Other than family, religion is the most important element of Nepalese society and the daily life of the country's people. It is a beautiful and complex tapestry that has been shaped by many influences. In Nepal, Hinduism, Buddhism, and several other religious beliefs have been intertwined to create a faith that is unique to the country. Most people, for example, openly practice traits associated with both Buddhism and Hinduism. Nepal is unique in that few countries can match its religious harmony and tolerance.

Nepalese people worship different gods and goddesses at different times, and for a variety of reasons. Each family may

The biggest and longest festival in Nepalese culture, Dashain lasts
15 days and commemorates the victory of the gods over demons.
On the tenth day, family elders bless their relatives by applying *tikas,*
ceremonial red spots, on the foreheads of everyone in the family.

select one or more gods or goddesses as a special family deity
for daily worship. Brahma, Vishnu, and Shiva are the main gods.
Krishna, Rama, Devi Durga, Kali, Laxmi, and Sarashwati are the
other forms of gods and goddesses. Laxmi is the goddess of
wealth, and Sarashwati is the goddess of learning. Vishnu is the
preserver of all creatures, and he is believed to have 10 different
incarnations, including Rama, Krishna, and Buddha. Each deity
or god receives a special form of worship, which is celebrated as
a festival. There are many such occasions each year.

Dashain is Nepal's most important festival. It is celebrated
by Hindus during the autumn as a day of victory over demons.
In general, Dashain is celebrated for 15 days. The first nine
days are called Navaratri, a period of worship during which
gods are called upon to assist in the battle against demons.

On the tenth day, there is a celebration of triumph over evil. The elderly person of the household puts a *tika* (ceremonial red spot) on the forehead of all persons in the family, with blessings and the exchange of gifts. During the final five days, people celebrate by visiting relatives to receive tikas and blessings of the goddess Durga.

5

Government and Politics

I n 1960, after a decade of political unrest, King Mahendra seized
control of the government. King Mahendra banned political parties and allowed autocratic rule through a group of councils, or
panchayats. Although the people did not have a say in their own government, the social reforms adopted by the king and the panchayats
did help alleviate some caste discrimination.

THE MONARCHY

The notion of absolute monarchy is actually a young concept.
The Nepalese monarchy as we know it is only about 250 years old;
whereas, the United Kingdom traces its history of a ruling monarchy
to the ninth century. There were rulers of separate areas, called Malla
kings; in A.D. 1200, however, after almost 600 years they were not

united and in the late eighteenth century Prithvi Narayan Shah, king of Gorkha, conquered Kathmandu and united Nepal into one kingdom.

There was a brief movement toward a constitutional monarchy from 1951 to 1960, when the Nepalese people rose up against feudal autocracy, but that was quickly quashed after many struggles between King Mahendra and the Nepalese Congress Party who were supposed to be corulers. The panchayat system governed Nepal until 1989, when the People's Movement forced the monarchy to accept constitutional reforms and to establish a multiparty Parliament.

A NEW CONSTITUTION

In 1990, Nepal adopted a new constitution that established a multiparty democracy, ending 30 years of absolute rule. Faced with major pro-democracy protests by the banned political parties, King Birendra agreed to large political reforms. While the king maintained significant powers as head of state, a prime minister would be head of the government. The legislature was bicameral (two-chamber) consisting of a national council (Rashtriya Sabha) and a house of representatives (Pratinidhi Sabha) that is directly elected by the people. All Nepali citizens can vote when they turn 18. The executive branch consisted of the king and the Council of Ministers (the Cabinet). The cabinet was appointed by the king and the prime minister.

These political changes were recognized as a victory of "good people for good system" over "bad system." A crucial shift in the Nepalese way of thinking contributed to the reconstruction of Nepal's social structure. Equal opportunity was provided to all people, and education was free. For the first time, female participation in political activities was encouraged, and quotas in Parliament for women were instated.

The political changes in 1990 established a new constitution that included reforms to legislature, voting laws, and the executive branch of government. Women were granted access to political activities, and a quota was established to ensure female participation in Parliament. As the Speaker of the Nepalese lower House Parliament, Chitralekha Yadav *(above)* is the highest-ranking female in the Nepalese government.

THE PEOPLE'S WAR

Nepal's citizens had high expectations. Over time, people became disenchanted with the pace and direction of change. In 1994, a radical leftist party called the Communist Party of Nepal-Maoist (CPN-M) was formed, led by Pushpa Kamal Dahal, a Brahmin of modest means from the Chitwa District. In 1996, CPN-M, or the Maoists, presented a list of 40 demands related to "nationalism, democracy, and livelihood," including the elimination of discriminatory treaties such as the 1950 Nepal-India Treaty, which controlled the distribution of water and electricity and the delineation of the border between the two countries. They also thought that land should be confiscated from the rich and redistributed to the poor. When their demands were not met, they declared war on the government. The People's War was aimed at overthrowing the government, doing away with the monarchy, and establishing a people's republic.

THE ROYAL MASSACRE

During this time of political instability and a declining economy, in June 2001, the nation was shocked by the massacre of King Birendra and eight members of the royal family. Although an official investigation concluded that the king's son Prince Dipendra had killed his family members in a drunken rage before committing suicide, the general public remains skeptical. King Birendra reigned for almost 20 years and was highly respected for being liberal and turning over the government to a multiparty democracy. After Birendra's death, his younger brother, Gyanendra, inherited the throne. Known as a hardliner and a businessman, King Gyanendra dissolved the multiparty government and assumed full executive powers in order to fight the Maoists in 2005.

The civil war disrupted the majority of rural activities that had been established with the new constitution. The government controlled the main cities and towns while the Maoists seized control of small villages. Civilians were affected most by the violence, with attacks being made on them by government troops and Maoist rebels. Besides attacking police stations and district headquarters, the Maoists placed bombs in schools, blockaded roads and passenger vehicles (limiting the movement of commerce and necessary products), and attacked people who defied the ban on working. At the same time, the government suspended many constitutional rights and freedoms by banning all provocative statements about the monarchy, imprisoning journalists, and shutting down newspapers. Although the Royal Nepal Army was not involved in the war at first, after the Maoists attacked an army barracks, the army assaulted the insurgents and anyone they thought was

King Birendra *(sitting left)*, the monarch who had reintroduced true democracy to Nepal, was killed along with seven other members of the royal family when his son Dipendra *(center)* murdered them before killing himself. Birendra's death led to the ascension of Gyanendra, his younger brother.

sympathetic to the cause. During this time, the king received aid from foreign countries.

During this decade-long civil war, nearly 13,000 people were killed, and 100,000 to 150,000 Nepalese were internally displaced. As a result, the tourism industry, Nepal's greatest source of revenue, decreased significantly. Once ranked tenth on a list of iExplore's (a travel company's) published reports based on sales, Nepal moved to twenty-seventh in 2005. Young people also moved out of the country, seeking employment and stability in neighboring countries. They found employment in Middle East countries like Qatar and Saudi Arabia, and in Southeast Asia. Their families are heavily dependent upon the money they send back home. This foreign income has permitted the country to avoid a serious economic crisis.

Cease-fires and negotiations were initiated several times during the war, to no avail. In April 2006, hundreds of thousands of people protested through the streets of Kathmandu against autocratic rule. In response, government troops fired into crowds, killing more than a dozen people. Faced with daily protests, a general strike, and roadblocks that cut off the city from fuel and food supplies, King Gyanendra restored Parliament, which he had suspended four years earlier, and named Girija Prasad Koirala as prime minister. Using its newfound authority, the House of Representatives stripped the king of his power and declared Nepal a secular state. The Maoist rebels declared a three-month truce and began peace talks with the government.

In November 2006, the Maoist rebels reached a peace agreement with the Nepalese government. As part of the agreement, the Maoists, under United Nations supervision, turned over their weapons and limited their troops to camps. For the government's part, a commission was set up to investigate human rights abuses by both sides in the long conflict. Maoists joined the government in April 2007 after Prime Minister Koirala assigned 5 of the 22 cabinet posts to the CPN (Maoists).

The government planned to take over the monarch's assets while allowing Gyanendra to keep property he owned before he inherited the throne.

Democratic elections for a constituent assembly were scheduled for June 2007. On schedule was the creation of a new constitution and the decision to remain a monarchy or become a republic. However, the elections were subsequently postponed due to new demands by the Maoists. They required the abolition of the monarchy before the elections and the implementation of a balanced voting system for the elections. Although all of the political parties in the interim government agreed on ending the monarchy, the new demands contradicted the earlier agreement. The two groups came to a political deadlock. Elections were further delayed when the Maoists withdrew from the governing coalition in September 2007.

In December 2007, Parliament passed a bill that declared Nepal a constitutionally "federal democratic republic." The bill, however, will not take effect until after the elections of April 2008.

MODERN POLITICAL PARTIES

Since the late 1940s, the struggle for control has been a contest between three organizations: the Nepali Congress Party (NCP), the Communist Party of Nepal (Unified Marxist-Leninist, or CPN-UML), and the royalist Rashtriya Prajatantra Party (RPP, also called the National Democratic Party). These three parties have gone through various incarnations as a result of political unrest. In 1998, a faction broke away from the CPN-UML and formed a new party, the Communist Party of Nepal (Marxist-Leninist), or CPN-ML. That same year, the National Democratic Party also split into two groups, with the formation of the National Democratic Party (Chand). In 2002, a breakaway faction of the NCP created the Nepali Congress Democrat, or NCD.

Historically, the Nepali Congress, a moderate socialist party, has advocated constitutional monarchy instead of absolute monarchy. Recently, the party has accepted the idea of a republic. On September 25, 2007, the Nepali Congress Party and the Nepali Congress Democrat unified and became a single party, the Nepali Congress. Girija Prasad Koirala, Krishna Prasad Bhattarai, and Sher Bahadur Deuba are the three senior leaders, with Koirala serving as the party's president.

The Communist Party of Nepal (Marxist-Leninist) was established in 1949. In the 1960s and 1970s, the party splintered into a number of different factions, eventually becoming the Communist Party of Nepal (Unified Marxist-Leninist, a moderate sector) and the Communist Party of Nepal (Unity Center, a more radical sector). The CPN-UC divided again and formed another party, the CPN (Maoist). Today, the Communist Party consists of the CPN (UML), the CPN (Maoist), and several smaller Communist groups. Five of these smaller groups have representation in Parliament.

With the new constitution in 1990, which installed multiparty democracy, the royalist party was formed. The Rashtriya Prajatantra Party, or RPP, became the third most important group in parliamentary politics during the 1990s. This promonarchy party was created from the elite panchayat system. In 1997, the RPP split and a faction joined a coalition government with the CPN (UML). Those left behind in the RPP allied themselves with the Nepali Congress and dismantled the UML-RPP, making two separate royalist coalition parties. In 1998, the parties unified after a bad showing in the elections that year, but the party split again into the Rashtriya Janashakti Party, or RJP. Today the RPP and the RJP are both represented in Parliament.

6

Nepal's Economy

By nearly any measure, Nepal ranks as one of the world's poorest countries. It, like many African and several other Asian states, is undergoing a huge cultural and economic transition. Most Nepalese—about four of every five—continue to live in the country, where they practice a very traditional lifestyle. Most survive on a subsistence economy. They raise their own food, build their own homes, and otherwise provide for the majority of their material needs. What they cannot grow or make, they trade for in an ancient barter system, in remote villages. They are independent, largely self-sufficient, and proud. Only about 20 percent of the rural homes have electricity, and few have modern indoor plumbing.

Geographers refer to such a lifestyle as a *folk culture*. Such people work long, hard hours, but little of what they do "counts" in monetary terms, the way economies are measured today. They may live very well by the standards of their own culture and country. Yet, because they work in a subsistence, rather than cash, economy, they are considered (statistically) to be "poor." Their worldview may extend no farther than the horizon they can see from their home. These people live in what are called less-developed countries (LDCs). In terms of income, a comparison between the Nepalese and residents of the United States or Canada is revealing. The per capita income in Nepal is less than $400 a year. This means that a typical Nepalese makes only about one percent as much as a resident of Northern America. Looking at it another way, they make less in one year than most workers in developed countries make in a single week.

Only about 16 percent of Nepal's population is urban. Most of these people, like the great majority of Americans and Canadians, live in a modern, industrial, or service-oriented cash economy. They go to work, earn wages, and, with their income, purchase the goods and services that they need. Such people are outward looking. They are much more "worldly" in terms of trade, communications, information, travel, and their view of their global neighbors. It is in this context—the vast differences that separate Nepal's rural and urban populations—that this chapter is set.

GOVERNMENT AND ECONOMY

A very close relationship exists between a country's government and its economy. In Chapter 3, you learned how chaotic Nepal's government has been throughout the country's history. As a result, economic development has lagged. If, on the other hand, an economy is weak, a government will not have the revenue it needs for development and to provide essential services. It works both ways. Because of poor government and a weak economy, Nepal remains one of the world's least developed countries. In fact, on the United Nation's (UN) Human Development Index (HDI), Nepal ranks 142nd

Turbulent government reforms, limited resources, and a long conflict with Maoist rebels have prevented economic and social development in Nepal. Poor families like the Dalits *(above)* rely on an agricultural way of life, and their two cows are their most valuable possessions.

among the 177 countries ranked. With the exception of Haiti, it is the lowest ranked of any country in the world outside of Africa. The HDI takes a number of factors into consideration when determining its rankings, including education, literacy, life expectancy, and standard of living. It is the primary source of information used by many individuals and agencies that classify countries as being developed, developing, or less developed.

PRIMARY INDUSTRIES

Primary industries are those that involve the extraction and use of natural resources. They include such activities as agriculture, mining, logging, and fishing. Today, most countries—particularly those considered to be developed—rely on primary industries for just a small fraction of their gross domestic product (GDP). In the United States and Canada, for example, less than 2 percent of the GDP comes from primary industrial activities. In Nepal, the figure is 38 percent from agriculture alone. Another revealing figure is productivity. In both the United States and Canada, less than one percent of the population is engaged in primary economic activities, but their productivity is greater than their number. In Nepal, on the other hand, nearly 80 percent of the population depends upon agriculture—but farming and herding contribute only 38 percent of the country's GDP. This means that Nepal's rural people are quite unproductive economically relative to their numbers. It also suggests that most farming is for subsistence only and that, by and large, practices are quite inefficient. This situation, however, is very typical of a traditional folk society.

Agriculture

Traditional agricultural methods have changed little since ancient times. Nepalese peasants utilize small parcels of land, which are passed down from generation to generation through inheritance, to feed their families. They primarily grow staple foods such as rice, wheat, and corn, and root crops, most of which is used for human subsistence or livestock. Commercial and industrial crops include sugarcane, jute (a fiber), and tobacco. Livestock products include water buffalo meat and milk. Most of the country's agriculture is in the warm, moist, lowland plains of the Terai region.

Agriculture in local villages is a family activity in which children help their parents at all stages—from tilling the fields and planting to harvesting. In a good year, when surpluses are available, peasants exchange grain for other goods that are manufactured by their neighbors. Sometimes they travel to a local market, where they can acquire clothes, tools, and other materials in exchange for their own products. In this cultural environment, bartering is the key to everyday survival.

Today, Nepal, like many other less developed countries, is undergoing gradual change. The influence of globalization is increasing, and its impact is being felt on even the smallest and most remote countries. Times have long passed when a place could remain isolated from others. In this context, the Nepalese economy, as minor as it is, will eventually enter the market system. Step by step, traditional economies will be replaced by a commercially oriented market economy, even in the most remote villages. This trend is already visible in the shrinking influence of agriculture in the country's gross domestic product. A country such as Nepal cannot rely on its own commercial agriculture to provide the nation's needs. Self-sufficiency is costly to achieve and technologically difficult to develop in a poor country. As a result, Nepal is dependent on imports for much of its food, particularly that consumed in urban centers. Such an economic policy, however, creates several problems.

First, the imported products lower prices of and demand for locally grown crops. This, in turn, decreases the already low incomes of Nepalese peasants. Second, such economic maneuvering decreases the need for labor and contributes to the growth of unemployment. Finally, high unemployment rates lead to a variety of serious social issues and unrest. This is a "catch-22" for the developing world. Such countries need to modernize in order to achieve long-term economic benefits. In so doing, however, governments in the LDCs often create a number of short-term problems. In Nepal, where so many people are tied to the land, this problem is of substantial magnitude. To prevent potential economic, social, and political problems, various attempts have been made to develop the country's agricultural sector. With help from international institutions and agencies, several projects have been envisioned. Progress, however, has been very slow, and the impact on the national economy has been minimal.

Mining

Nepal has a variety of mineral resources, but most are found in deposits so small, or so remote from transportation facilities, that they are not worth exploiting. The primary commercial mining operations extract marble, limestone, talc, and magnesite (used in steelmaking). There are small deposits of cobalt, copper, lead, and zinc, and some placer gold is extracted from stream gravels. Building materials include stone, sand, gravel, and clay. Although small deposits of coal and natural gas exist, nearly all fossil fuel resources must be imported. Some precious stones, such as garnet, ruby, tourmaline, beryl, and aquamarine, also have been found.

Logging

There is very little commercial logging in Nepal. The cutting of woodlands, however, is widespread. Wood is used in construction and as fuel. As a result of excessive deforestation, flooding and landslides have become increasingly commonplace. Some scientists, in fact, blame the cutting removal of woodlands for the massive flooding that occurs in Nepal. Rainfall runs down cleared deforested slopes much more rapidly than off those on which forests remain intact. Water from both snowmelt and monsoon rains arrive in early summer. This runoff moisture gathers rapidly in tributaries to the Ganges (Ganga) River. Soon, the Ganges, itself, swells with floodwater. Eventually, it joins the Brahmaputra River in Bangladesh (which flows from the heavily deforested northern slopes of the Himalayas). During periods of extreme flooding, as much as two-thirds of Nepal is severely affected.

Hydroelectric Power

Many Nepalese (and others) foresee hydroelectric power generation as the country's most obvious potential source of economic growth. Mountainous landscapes, high amounts of annual precipitation, and dozens of fast-flowing streams create an ideal environment for power plants. Furthermore, Nepal's geographic location—in this context, at least—is a real blessing. It has as neighbors the world's two most heavily populated countries and lands that rank among the world's most rapidly growing economies. India and China are hungry for any kind of energy to fuel their future economic growth and development. Both could be major customers for Nepal's surplus electrical energy.

Economic reports estimate that currently only one to two percent of Nepal's hydroelectric potential has been harnessed. The main issue here, as in many other aspects of Nepal's economy, is the removal of large-scale projects from direct governmental control. In less developed countries, political leadership often relates economic progress with its own benefits. As a result, governments maintain strict control over many revenue-producing activities (such as energy production) and financial management. In other words, corruption must be eliminated in order to attract foreign investments. Nepal is no exception.

SECONDARY INDUSTRIES

During recent decades, globalization has created some rather peculiar economic trends. For example, a number of countries have managed to transform their economy from agriculture based to service oriented in a relatively short period of time. In so doing, they have almost entirely bypassed manufacturing. That is, they have jumped over the secondary stage of industrial development. If Nepal is to join the economically developed world, this fast-forward scenario is both necessary and quite possible. Manufacturing industries barely exist in Nepal. In other words, the country has not made the transition from primary to secondary economic activity and dependence.

For example, only about 20 percent of the country's $41 billion GDP was contributed by the manufacturing sector—or about $8 billion. This sector is by no means Nepal's equivalent to the glory days of Detroit or Pittsburgh in the United

Bhaktapur is the city in Nepal known for manufacturing pottery, woodcarvings, weavings, and various traditional art items that can be found in Asian markets. The country's manufacturing industry is woefully underdeveloped, as globalization has encouraged the Nepalese economy to focus on the service sector.

States. Most companies are small, and production revolves around products Western customers admire during visits to Oriental market stores. Very few manufactured goods are exported. Those that are include carpets, textiles, clothing, and leather goods.

TERTIARY INDUSTRIES

Tertiary industries are those associated with the provision of services. They include professionals such as teachers, attorneys, and people working in the provision of health and medical assistance. Sales, mid-level management, communications, and transportation also fall within the service sector. In most developed countries today, the overwhelming majority of the GDP is generated by tertiary industries. In the developed world, about 70 to 80 percent of a country's GDP is generated by service-related activities. In Nepal, the figure is about 42 percent.

Until recent decades, the service sector of Nepal's economy was very poorly developed. Today, however, this is changing. In fact, there is ample room for optimism as the service sector experiences encouraging growth. Globalization, in the form of local entrepreneurs, has managed to reach even the most isolated villagers. For example, there are more than one million cellular phones in use in the country. In recent years, expansion of cellular-phone-providing services has more than doubled. Between 2000 and 2005, the number of Nepalese with direct access to telephone service increased from 11 per 1,000 to 25 per 1,000. Additionally, remote communities may have several television sets linked to satellite dishes. In 2006, only a quarter-million Nepalese were Internet users, but access certainly will increase in the future. The number of Internet users, although miniscule, has more than doubled during the past several years. These windows to the world require managers, installers and repairmen, secretaries, accountants, and others.

Such service-related projects begin in urban centers and gradually spread into the countryside. Before they know it, peasants enjoy the luxury of contemporary living, even though roads are not yet paved and the only transportation device has four legs. A year or so later, this will change as well. There are only so many cellular phones that can be sold. Thus, local junior venture capitalists may indeed create another project that will require employing even more people. Roads may be paved in order to build a bank, school, or industry. Access and accommodations such as lodging and dining facilities need to be built for tourists who want to see or climb the country's majestic mountains. This is how the service sector develops, slowly and often painfully, in countries such as Nepal.

Economic analysts, both domestic and foreign, believe that the development of Nepal's service sector, if ultimately successful, must emphasize the growth of tourism. The country has astoundingly beautiful natural landscapes, highlighted by the world's most spectacular mountain peaks. It has tremendous cultural diversity and attractive rural cultural landscapes. Many Nepalese support the development of tourism, which they believe to be a "clean" industry. For many decades, a few people came to the country each year to climb Mount Everest. To most outsiders, perhaps that seemed to be the only place worth visiting, or thing to do. With development of a tourist infrastructure, many argue, Nepal has the potential to become the "Switzerland of the Himalayas." Who could argue against that?

The service sector depends on a reliable banking system. It must provide adequate financial support for expansion and also accommodate potential foreign investments. Nepal's financial sector is in desperate need of liberalization and expansion of services. Fortunately, it is being assisted by the World Bank and other international institutions. Currently, only about a quarter of households enjoy the luxury of banking, holding an account into which they can deposit or from which they can withdraw money. For two of every four Nepalese, economic transactions between people must rely on some other means of exchange. This is typical of a folk culture in which barter, rather than currency, is the primary medium of exchange.

TRANSPORTATION AND INFRASTRUCTURE

In a folk culture, people do not travel far from their village unless they are a nomadic population that follows their herds of livestock. Most residents of permanent villages spend their entire lifetime in or very near their place of birth. Travel away from the village where they are born may be only to seek medical help or for religious purposes, such as participating in a pilgrimage. Leisure travel is a totally foreign experience for most villagers (people living in a folk culture) worldwide. It is often said that "the folk never travel farther than the horizon that they can see at birth."

Until recently, Nepal's rural environment remained little changed from what it was like many generations ago. Outside of Kathmandu and several other larger communities, few permanent trails existed, and those were often in very rough condition. The quality of mountain "highways" depended on how difficult it was to pass by foot, or on the back of a domestic animal. Suspension bridges over rapid, deep canyons had no rest areas from which to admire views.

If Nepal is to modernize, it will require extensive and extremely costly improvements in the country's transportation infrastructure. Without any major connections to the world, the need for such a project has never been more urgent. Both political stability and economic development depend on reliable and extensive transportation linkages. You may have heard the expression, "All roads lead to Rome." The vast Roman Empire was able to maintain itself because it had well-developed links to all regions under its control. In the absence of such linkages, remote areas are often subject to terrorist activity, secessionist movements, and guerrilla warfare.

This has been a problem for Nepal in the past, including during the Maoist movement of the past decade. If transportation networks are well developed, uprisings can be easily subdued because troops and goods can be moved rapidly around a country's territory. In Nepal, it is critical that connections between Kathmandu and the countryside be greatly improved. This would facilitate economic development and help the peripheral areas to catch up with the cities.

Isolation can breed dissatisfaction and unrest. This is something that Nepal, so often torn apart by internal strife, can ill afford. Many of Nepal's prospects for future economic development also depend on improved access. Today, only about one-third of the country's population has access to all-weather roads. Nearly all of them, however, are located in the Terai lowlands and mountain foothills. More than half of the country has almost no access whatsoever. Nepal's landlocked position and rugged terrain create many additional obstacles.

The country has only 10,800 miles (17,380 kilometers) of roadway, about half of which is paved. Amazingly, it has only about 37 miles (59 kilometers) of railroad, some of which is managed by an Indian company. There are hardly any waterways that can be navigated by boats other than small rafts and other sport craft. As an exit to the global sea, Nepal uses the Indian port of Calcutta (Kolkata). Air traffic projects a slightly brighter picture, although it, too, is in serious need of improvement. The international airport in Kathmandu serves as the main hub for domestic air travel and is the sole hub for international connections.

TOURISM

In Nepal, tourism really did not begin until 1953. In that year, a New Zealand mountaineer and explorer named Sir Edmund Hillary, guided by his Sherpa assistant, Tenzing Norgay, stood atop Mount Everest. They were the first climbers to achieve this monumental feat; generations of professional and amateur climbers would follow their footsteps. A quarter century later, Italian climber Reinhold Messner and his Austrian partner, Peter Habler, would accomplish the previously unthinkable. They reached the summit without an additional oxygen supply. The interest in conquering physical extremes, such as the world's

There have been about 1,200 successful attempts to scale Mount Everest since Sir Edmund P. Hillary and Tenzing Norgay climbed to the summit over 50 years ago, as ordinary people strive to achieve their dream of conquering this extraordinary peak. Technology and mountaineering classes have made the mountain more accessible to climbers, though the price for such an expedition, along with a personal Sherpa guide, can run up to $65,000 and more.

highest peaks, will always attract adventurers. Today, Nepal generates a sizable profit from those who seek such challenges.

Because of its diverse environments, Nepal offers a variety of challenging options for those who seek a thrill, or just an opportunity to do something different. Some tourists seeking adventure come to climb or hike the high Himalayas. Others are attracted by the country's fast-rushing mountain streams. They come to Nepal to kayak or raft some of the world's most challenging waters. In the steaming tropical lowlands, jungle safaris are a popular tourist attraction. Treks through the Himalayas are particularly popular, especially among Westerners who can afford the luxury of international leisure activities. All tourism, however, brings in much-needed foreign currency. Unfortunately, Nepal's tourist sector still lacks the capacity to accommodate large-scale luxury tourism. Most tourists are limited to climbing, hiking, visiting villages, and observing customs, all with a minimum amount of traditional service offerings. Thus, tourists do not have an opportunity to spend larger sums of money as they no doubt would do elsewhere.

During the past decade, Nepal's attempts to increase its visibility as a major tourist destination have been thwarted. Political upheaval related to the Maoist uprising was partially to blame. The lack of foreign investments designed to promote the development of tourist facilities also hindered growth in this sector of the economy. Following the end of the conflict, conditions have begun to improve. Since 2006, international arrivals, supported particularly from Europe and East Asia, have increased by about 25 percent. Today, the number of visitors is approaching a half million each year. Tourism employs about 250,000 people and has become Nepal's third-largest source of revenue.

LABOR AND TRADE

Economic accomplishments cannot occur without a skillful and well-educated workforce. Nepal's economy is in desperate need of a better-trained labor pool. This situation is commonplace within LDCs—the transition from a "jack-of-all-trades, master-of-none" folk culture and traditional economy to the demands of a contemporary economy is huge. In the modern world, one must be able to read and write to be successful, yet fewer than half of all Nepalese are literate. New skills must be learned, and new attitudes toward wealth and its accumulation must be developed. Such changes often take many generations to accomplish successfully.

Young people, in particular, are challenged by the transition from folk to contemporary popular culture. Today, they account for about one-half of the country's unemployed. At the same time, one-third of the population lives below the poverty line. Among the many challenges that the Nepalese government faces, none is greater than improving the country's educational system. An educated workforce is essential if a country is to successfully undertake the change from a traditional economy to one based on information and providing services.

As one would expect, keeping in mind close geographical and cultural ties between nations, India is Nepal's major trade partner. In regard to both categories, exports and imports, the economic exchange with India accounts for two-thirds of Nepal's foreign trade, a figure that continues to increase annually. Unfortunately, the trade balance between the two countries has reached seriously negative proportions. As a result, Nepal is experiencing and suffering from an expanding foreign debt. In recent years, the size of imports has exceeded exports by a margin of two to one. With the United States, nevertheless, Nepal has established a positive trade balance, with 11.7 percent of its total exports and miniscule imports.

CHAPTER

7

Living in
Nepal Today

Considering its relatively small size, few of the world's countries can match Nepal for its regional diversity. Physically,
it varies from hot, subtropical lowlands to towering, ice-
capped peaks. Culturally, it offers one of the world's most complex
mosaics of languages, religions, and customs. In this chapter, cities
are emphasized in the context of highlighting Nepal's various regions.
As is true of all regional divisions, those discussed here have been
selected arbitrarily. Sharp regional boundaries rarely exist, whether
physically or culturally. This makes it very difficult to draw regional
"lines" on which everyone can agree.

Nepal's historical record, some of which may be based on myths,
mentions ancient cities. Some, such as Janakpur and Biratnagar, may
be more than 1,000 years old—older than Kathmandu. Janakpur is
believed to have been the capital of the Mithila Kingdom ruled by

King Janak. Similarly, Biratnagar is thought to have been the capital of the Birat Kingdom ruled by King Birat. Kathmandu is said to have come into existence when Manjushree visited the Kathmandu Valley and drained the water out of the then-existing lake. He established a city called Manjupattan and settled Buddhist disciples in the valley. The Kirat Dynasty started its regime in the Kathmandu Valley in about 800 B.C. The Shakya Dynasty (ruled by King Shuddhodhan, the father of Gautama Buddha) had its heyday in and around Lumbini (the birthplace of Buddha) in approximately 600 B.C. Thus, the development of cities and the civilizations that grew around them took place gradually. Eventually, some emerged as major population, economic, and administrative centers.

Today, there are a number of cities scattered throughout much of the country. Each of them has achieved its own unique historical and geographical importance, including its social, religious, and economic role. Among the cities, Kathmandu is Nepal's capital and largest urban center. It is one of five major cities located within the Kathmandu Valley. There are a total of 58 municipalities in Nepal. This designation, as well as others that classify communities, is based on population and other factors such as culture and economy. The heart of the country is the Kathmandu Valley, so we will begin our tour of Nepal's cities and regions there.

CITIES OF THE KATHMANDU VALLEY

The Kathmandu Valley is the heart and soul of Nepal. Physically, it is a bowl-shaped feature located at an elevation of about 4,600 feet (1,400 meters) in central Nepal's hill district. When flying, it gives one a strange feeling to be airborne above the valley floor, but surrounded by higher hilltops and mountain peaks. The documented history of the Kathmandu Valley goes back to ancient times. According to legend a Buddhist saint, Manjushree, drained the huge lake occupying the valley, thereby making the valley floor habitable. Followers of

Most of Nepal's urban population lives in the capital, Kathmandu, which is located in the Kathmandu Valley. Shaped like a bowl and rich in culture and tradition, visiting the valley is recommended for everyone considering a trip to Nepal.

Buddhism settled in the valley, perhaps as early as the fifth century B.C. Over time, urban centers like Kathmandu, Patan, and Bhaktapur were settled and grew. Each of them evolved its own distinct culture, including language, architecture, and a unique synthesis of Hinduism and Buddhism.

Today, the Kathmandu Valley is the major center of population, government, economic activity, and culture. A number of the cultural heritage sites within the Kathmandu Valley are world famous. In fact, of Nepal's 10 UN World Heritage Sites, 7 are located within the Kathmandu Valley. They include monuments and old buildings such as palaces, temples, and *stupas* (a Buddhist religious structure). Among them, the palaces include Hanuman Dhoka (Kathmandu), Patan Dhoka Darbar Square, and Bhaktapur Darbar Square; Hindu temples include Pashupatinath and Changunarayan; and Buddhist stupas include Swayambhunath and Buddhanath. The Kathmandu Valley offers an incredible array of Buddhist shrines and Hindu temples, making the area an open museum.

Over time, the local Newar people created a unique culture in their valley homeland. Many visitors have admired their art, architecture, and lifestyle. Some have commented that "every other building is a temple and every other day is a festival." Among the festivals celebrated in Nepal, Gai Jatra, Ghode Jatra, Red Machhindra Jatra, Maha Shivaratri, and Buddha Jayanti are the most popular in the Kathmandu Valley.

Kathmandu

Kathmandu (previously named Kantipur) is the major social, cultural, political, and economic hub, as well as the first entry point of most tourists entering the country. Nepal's only international airport is centrally located in the Kathmandu Valley. The city is rich in ancient cultures, traditions, and buildings. The prevailing lifestyle, ceremonies, old temples, buildings, and monuments reflect the richness of a tradition blended in Hinduism and Buddhism. Kathmandu is known as the "City of the Gods." Therefore, the city's major tourist attractions are religious structures such as temples, shrines, and monuments.

At the very heart of Kathmandu is Hanuman Dhoka Darbar Square. This ancient square includes a complex of palaces (including Kumari Ghar, home of the living goddess Kumari), courtyards, temples, and a museum. Most structures were built between the twelfth and eighteenth centuries. Hanuman Dhoka Palace was the main political center and residence of the king before Narayanhiti Royal Palace was constructed. This palace is still important because of its historical traditions, and most important state social, religious, and political ceremonies are performed here.

The valley offers excellent scenery, including picturesque views of Manaslu, Gorakh, Everest, and other peaks. A combination of historical, cultural, and natural features in and surrounding Kathmandu have contributed to the city's charm. The myths and legends, religious traditions and mysticism, reverence and meditation combine to make Kathmandu a magically romantic place. It is said that the name Kathmandu was taken from Kasthamandap (a temple of wood), which was made from a single tree in the pagoda style in A.D. 1596. Thamel is the main tourist hot spot. Nightlife there has a strongly Western (hip-hop) flavor, as it blends the tastes of Eastern and Western cultures. Hinduism's oldest and holiest temple, Pashupatinath, and the Buddhist shrines Swayambhu and Buddhanath are the most popular tourist spots in Kathmandu.

Lalitpur (Patan)

Lalitpur is believed to have been founded by the Kirat Dynasty in the third century B.C. Today, with a population of about 200,000, it is the second-largest city in the Kathmandu Valley and the third largest in Nepal. It is also a popular tourist destination. Lalitpur is located in the southeastern part of the valley, on the south side of the Bagmati River. During recent decades, the city has begun to merge with Kathmandu. Lalitpur is believed to be the oldest—and certainly the most beautiful—of the royal cities. It is famous for its fine arts and crafts, as well as its rich cultural heritage. The city has produced a number of well-known artists and craftsmen. Its palaces, temples, and stupas reflect the superb artistic excellence and craftsmanship of the local Newar people since ancient times. There are more than 1,200 Buddhist monuments and stupas in different shapes and sizes.

The artistic center of Nepal, Lalitpur, is located in the Kathmandu Valley and boasts the country's largest community of metal- and woodworkers. Filled with temples, monasteries, pagodas, and sacred buildings, Lalitpur is only about three miles (five kilometers) away from the capital and has become a popular tourist destination.

The Patan Durbar Square area includes most of the historical stupas and monuments. The square is also one of the seven World Heritage Sites in the Kathmandu Valley. Many beautiful stone-built Hindu temples, such as the temple of Krishna, reveal the marvelous craftsmanship of the valley's seventeenth-century builders. To many tourists visiting the city, all of Lalitpur appears to be an open museum of arts and crafts.

Pulchowki Mountain and the Royal Botanical Garden are also centers of interest for many visitors.

Bhaktapur (Bhadgaon)

The third royal city of the Kathmandu Valley, Bhaktapur, is renowned for its elegant art, culture, and lifestyle. Bhaktapur, a city of about 78,000 people, is known as the "City of Cultural Gems" and the "Living Heritage" for its majestic arts and craftsmanship, colorful festivals, and the traditional lifestyle of its people. Bhaktapur Durbar Square stands like an open museum displaying its superb ancient art and sculptures. A World Heritage Site, the square offers an assemblage of unique palaces, temples, and monasteries. Structures reflect an amazing array of skilled artwork on wood, metal, and stone. Most of the structures were built by Malla kings during the twelfth century. Each monument reflects the social outlook and religious beliefs of the society.

Bhaktapur contains several masterpieces of art. The world-famous Nyatapola Temple, Taleju Temple, 55-Window Palace, Golden Gate, and Peacock Window are among the city's many masterpieces that blend Hindu and Buddhist themes. They are famous for their artistically carved windows and doors. Furthermore, the mesmerizing natural scenery of the panoramic Himalayas steals the hearts of travelers and adds beauty to the city. The city is famous for its yogurt and a special type of cap worn by men called a *Bhaad-gaaule topi.*

Kirtipur

Kirtipur, recognized by Nepalese as "Glorious Town," is located in the southwestern part of the Kathmandu Valley. Kirtipur is spread out atop a hill, a position that has given the city several advantages. With a commanding view of the surrounding plains, Kirtipur occupies a strategic military site. The city's history includes several historic battles. Kirtipur also offers spectacular views of surrounding terrain. Both day and night, the site affords a magnificent view of the surrounding Kathmandu Valley and its cities. In addition, from its hilltop location, the Himalayas rise as an incredible panorama.

The main (older) city lies at the top of the hill and includes palaces, temples, stupas, courtyards, and wells. The old structures and carvings of the temples and stupas reflect the artistic skill of the local people. Parts of the original forts and walls can be seen along the foothills. Modern Kirtipur has been spread out along the foothills below the older part of the city. Nepal's oldest and largest center of higher learning, Tribhuvan University, is located in the city. It also is home to the country's largest and most comprehensive library.

Some two miles (four kilometers) southeast of Kirtipur is the historic and well-known town of Chovar, the site of Chovar Gorge. According to legend, this unique feature was cut by Manjushree to drain the lake that occupied the Kathmandu Valley floor during early times. Chovar, with its steep hillsides, also contains relics of several old walled fortifications. Old temples, stupas, and other buildings are historic artifacts that illustrate the artistic richness of the place. Chovar also offers a magnificent view of the Kathmandu Valley. This has been instrumental in the establishment of a growing tourist industry, including modern hotels, in the area.

OTHER CITIES

Pokhara lies about 124 miles west of Kathmandu, at the foot of the Himalayas. It is Nepal's major tourist center; the city offers a phenomenal view of snow-capped Annapurna and other ranges. Most major trekking (hiking) routes to the Himalayas, including the world-famous Annapurna Circuit trek, radiate outward from Pokhara. As a result, the city has become the primary takeoff point for trekkers and other adventurers. Annapurna Circuit and Sanctuary, Dhawalagiri Around, Annapurna Base Camp, Jomsom Muktinath Trek, and Ghandruk-Ghorepani are the most famous trek routes around Pokhara.

There are many other tourist attractions in the vicinity of Pokhara, including the Phewa, Begnas, and Rupa lakes; Mahendra Cave; Devis Falls; and Seti Gandaki Gorge. The Seti River passes through the city and, amazingly, flows completely underground—beneath the community—throughout much of its course. It is often said that Pokhara "floats like a boat" above the Seti. Other popular tourist activities in the area include boating, swimming in lakes, golfing, microlight flights, and whitewater rafting. Many tourists take the short hike to nearby Sarangkot, a beautiful village located atop a low mountain. From this community, visitors have a spectacular view of Pokhara, Phewa Lake, and the Himalayas. In addition to enjoying the scenery, visitors can mingle with the local people and experience some of their culture, including local foods.

Janakpur

Janakpur is the capital of the ancient Mithila Kingdom, which is situated east of Kathmandu in the eastern Terai. Janakpur is the birthplace of Sita, the wife of Ayodhya King Ram (a legendary hero) who married Sita in the Janaki Temple. The famous Janaki Temple is located at the center of the city. Thousands of devotees come throughout the year to pay homage to Lord Ram and Sita. The annual grand ceremony is held during the festival of Bibah Panchami, which is celebrated as the wedding anniversary of Lord Ram and Goddess Sita. Lord Ram and Sita are two major characters of the great Hindu epic *Ramayan,* which deals with the victory over devils.

Lumbini

Lumbini is the birthplace of Guatama Buddha, the "Enlightened One" and founder of the Buddhist faith. The city, which lies south of the Kathmandu Valley, is a place that evokes feelings of spirituality, reverence, and devotion for thousands of faithful every year. No place is more holy than the Sacred Garden located at the site of Buddha's birth. The garden covers about three square miles (eight square kilometers) of the city. The garden's main attraction is the Mayadevi Temple, which was built in the exact spot where Buddha was born. (The location was discovered by a German archaeologist in 1895.) A sandstone sculpture portrays the scenes of Buddha's birth.

Ashoka Pillar is another Lumbini attraction. The great Indian emperor Ashoka visited Buddha's birthplace and was so impressed with the Buddha's growing fame that he erected a pillar to pay homage to him. Inscriptions carved on the pillar reveal its historic importance as the birthplace of Buddha. The Pushkarni pool, located alongside the Mayadevi Temple, is considered to be the holiest pool, where Prince Siddhartha had his first purification bath.

Today, the garden is a UNESCO World Heritage Site. This designation signifies the garden's historic, religious, architectural, and archaeological importance. The garden includes several temples, monasteries, and stupas established by many other countries, including Thailand, China, Myanmar, and Japan. As a result of the many sacred attractions, Lumbini has become one of the world's most important pilgrimage sites.

Chitwan District

Chitwan is a district in south-central Nepal, located about 90 miles (150 kilometers) south of the Kathmandu Valley. Bharatpur and Narayangadh are the major commercial and service centers of the region. The district is best known for the beautiful Royal Chitwan National Park (CNP), which was established in 1973 and made a World Heritage Site in 1984. Chitwan is home to a great variety of flora and fauna. It offers a wonderful opportunity to visitors who want to spot a tiger or rhino, or ride an elephant. In the past, Chitwan was protected as a massive hunting reserve for Ranas, who would invite European and Indian royalty and other foreign dignitaries to the area.

Over time, newly established settlements invaded the forested and hunting areas. Despite this encroachment, Chitwan still occupies more than 500 square miles (1300 square

Established in 1973, Chitwan National Park houses many different types of plant life, mammals, birds, and butterflies. The park also features some of the world's most endangered species, such as the Bengal tiger and the Asian rhinoceros, both of which can sometimes be seen on tourist safari trips.

kilometers) of virgin forest, swamps, and grasslands. The park itself is somewhat smaller, covering an area of 360 square miles (932 square kilometers). It provides shelter for hundreds of elephants, deer, water buffalo, single-horn rhinos, Royal Bengal tigers, leopards, crocodiles, and pythons. The CNP is home to about 43 species of mammals, 450 species of birds, and 45 species of amphibians and reptiles.

Birgunj

Birgunj is located in the southern Terai region, along Nepal's border with India. Because of its strategic position, the city has become the country's most important center of industry, trade, and commerce. Birgunj is the main entry point for all imported materials and tourists traveling on land; however, most overland visitors simply pass through on their way to destinations in Nepal or India.

Recently, a broad-gauge railroad linked Birgunj with India's rail network. This reflects the increasing importance of Birgunj as a strategic commercial and industrial junction for trade and commerce between Nepal and India, and beyond. In a very real sense, Birgunj is Nepal's gateway to the world. Almost 60 percent of the country's imports and exports pass through the city. Thus, Birgunj plays a very active role in the country's economic growth and development.

Located in the Terai region, Birgunj experiences high summer temperatures and very mild temperatures during the winter months. Because of its location, the city also offers a rich diversity of cultures and ethnic groups, including speakers of Nepali, Newari, Maithili, and Bhojpuri. Among the city's growing number of industries are those based upon agriculture and iron and steel production.

Nepalgunj

Nepalgunj, located in the western part of Nepal, is another important commercial center. Although it is located in the southwestern part of the Terai region, close to the Indian border, its economic influence reaches to the northern border with China. Nepalgunj provides all types of commercial and other services to western Nepal. It is an important regional hub for transportation and a center of education, health care, business, and more.

Nepalgunj is considered a gateway to some of the world's most exciting and scenic activities, including trekking routes into the Himalayas for adventurers. Nepalgunj is also home to people of many different cultures, including different languages and religions. The city has substantial numbers of Hindus, Buddhists, Muslims, and Christians. The Nepalgunj Medical College ensures that its people are provided with high-quality health care and educational opportunities. In addition, the Bardia National Park is major attraction located just a few miles from Nepalgunj.

Ilam

Ilam is located in the central part of the Ilam District, about 360 miles (600 kilometers) east of Kathmandu. Situated in the hill district adjacent to Nepal's eastern border, Ilam offers some of the country's most picturesque landscapes. As a backdrop, the majestic Mahabharat and Himalayan ranges tower above the surrounding hills, valleys, and striking agricultural landscapes. The region is perhaps best known for its scenic gardens that produce Nepal's best tea, which is a major export to European countries. In addition to tea, cardamom, ginger, and potatoes are major crops, and some milk is produced. Sandakpur, Shri Antu, and Mai Pokhari are popular tourist destinations. Shri Antu provides a splendid view of sunrises and sunsets, earning it the title of "Gem of Nepal." From Sandakpur, one has an astounding view of the eastern Himalayas stretching from Bhutan to Everest.

Muktinath/Jomsom

Muktinath lies above the clouds at an elevation of 12,300 feet (3,749 meters), about 11 miles (18 kilometers) northeast of Jomsom. It is a popular destination for tourists who are drawn by the area's magnificent scenery and diverse landscapes. The temple of Muktinath is situated on a high mountain range and can be visited during good weather. Jomsom, too, is a small village and a popular tourist destination. Tourists can reach Jomsom by a direct flight from Pokhara or, for the more adventurous, by trekking from Pokhara (or elsewhere). This trek is the oldest in the country. Known as the "classic" trek in Nepal, it follows a portion of the ancient trade route between India and Tibet. The major attractions are the Kaligandaki Valley, located between the soaring peaks of Dhaulagiri, Nilgiri, and Annapurna; the Muktinath Temple; and the Tibet-like country.

Namche Bazaar

Namche Bazaar is one of the most important villages for mountaineers and adventurers. It is located in the northeastern mountain region at an elevation of 11,286 feet (3,440 meters). The community is the gateway to the high Himalayas, including Mount Everest. All visitors trekking to the Khumbu region pass through Namche Bazaar. It is also an important stopover place for trekkers, whose bodies must become acclimatized to low oxygen levels before proceeding to a higher elevation. Additionally, Namche Bazaar is the main business center of the Khumbu region.

8

Nepal
Looks Ahead

Nepal's future has never looked brighter. The country continues to face many problems, but most of them can be resolved through time if the current wave of democracy continues to flow across the political landscape. Establishment of the Loktantric alliance in 2006 marked a turning point in Nepal's history. After centuries of oppressive government, the country now looks to the future with new inspiration and hope. Under their new government, the Nepalese people are eager to support a truly democratic system and to assign the worn-out and ragged hereditary rule to the dustbin of history. Nepalese were tremendously excited to have a citizen elected as the head of state after 240 years of hereditary royal control over the country and its people. For the first time in their history, in fact, the Nepalese people determined who would govern them.

After years fighting the Nepalese government and monarchy, Maoist rebels signed a cease-fire agreement in 2006 that has resulted in relatively calmer times for the country. Initially part of the parliamentary process, the rebels had grown tired of the maneuvering of politicians and took up arms to fight the government. After the cease-fire, the rebels have begun to take a more active role in the community and government, including starting up useful service projects, like a cleanup campaign *(above)*.

The year 2006 was important for another reason. In addition to the end of monarchial power, it marked the end of the decade-long Maoist uprising; the Maoists accepted the democratic process and became actively (and peacefully) involved in government activities. In 2007, the reinstated Parliament seized the power of the monarch and ended the king's status as the head of state. Although many problems remain to be ironed out, politically, Nepal's future looks brighter than ever. With political stability in place, the country can turn its attention to building a modern, developed, prosperous nation.

Nepal's physical environment will continue to be both a blessing and a curse. Its spectacular terrain offers a marvelous opportunity to further develop the tourist industry. Some will come simply to view the majestic mountains. Others will risk their lives to add their names to the growing number of people who have reached their summits. Many will come for the thrill of rafting some of the world's most challenging whitewater streams. Still others may want to visit the lush tropical land-scapes of the Terai lowland, perhaps to ride an elephant, or to see a tiger or rhino. Fast-rushing streams also give Nepal one of the world's greatest potential sources of hydroelectric development. Spatially, nearby energy-hungry India offers an eager and waiting market.

The mountainous terrain, of course, will continue to serve as a tremendous barrier to movement. Building roadways or railroads in rugged terrain is extremely costly and difficult. For decades to come, Nepal's various regions and many of its communities will continue to be relatively isolated from one another. This will help to retain the unique diversity of regional cultures and ethnic groups, but it will hinder economic growth and development.

Population will continue to plague the country's economic growth. Nepal has nearly 29 million people in an area approxi-mately the size of South Carolina (whose population equals about 4 million). Although all of South Carolina is inhabited, only about two-thirds of Nepal can support settlement. Nepal's population is growing by 2.1 percent each year, a full percent greater than the world average. In order to maintain or improve the country's standard of living, Nepal must ensure that its eco-nomic growth exceeds that of the population.

Nepal's cultural diversity also will continue to be both a source of conflict and a blessing. When the people within a country are culturally diverse, the different ways of living, thinking, and believing can lead to conflicts. The recent decade-long Maoist conflict was primarily fueled by rural, traditional societies rising up against the more affluent urban society. With several dominant religions, about 70 different languages, and many different ethnic groups, Nepal is faced with a serious challenge. How does a country ensure that its people think of themselves first as (in this case) Nepalese, and second as members of their tribal, ethnic, linguistic, or other group affiliation? Nepal will continue to have problems drawing its diverse people together and creating a Nepalese national identity.

Economic growth and development constitute a huge challenge to Nepal. The country continues to be dominantly rural, and the majority of its people continue to practice a subsistence folk economy. Meanwhile, neighboring India and China are experiencing tremendous economic growth. To catch up with them, Nepal must introduce many reforms, learn many lessons, and continue its current political stability. Political stability, peaceful conditions, and adequate security are keys to achieving economic development and prosperity.

Because of its past political situation, including the recent decade of Maoist terrorist activity, Nepal has attracted very little foreign investment. Even its own citizens have been reluctant to invest in their country. Hopefully, the situation will change under the current and future governments. If the economy is to grow, it is also essential that deep-rooted corruption be stopped. This will be difficult to accomplish, because it has become a way of life in the country. Corruption—hand in hand with conflict—has discouraged both foreign aid and international investments in Nepal.

Despite the many challenges that it faces, Nepal appears to be on the brink of a new age. Finally, it has achieved some semblance of political stability. This, in turn, will open the door to economic investment and development. Development of its massive hydroelectric potential can provide a tremendous boost to the country's economy. So, too, can expanded irrigation and crop production. It is, however, tourism that offers the greatest potential for future economic development. Wouldn't *you* like to visit the country to see its massive mountains, fast-flowing streams, and quaint villages? In order to make such a visit, though, you would first want to ensure that you would be safe. You would also expect to find an adequate infrastructure for tourism—lodging, restaurants, adequate transportation facilities, and so forth. Putting these things in place will take time and capital investment.

Now, for the first time ever, it appears that such a thing is possible.

Facts at a Glance

Note: All figures, unless otherwise indicated, are 2007 estimates.

Physical Geography

Location Southern Asia; situated between two huge countries: India to the east, south, and the west, and China to the north

Area Total: 56,827 square miles (147,181 square kilometers) Land: 55,282 square miles (143,181 square kilometers) Water: 1,544 square miles (4,000 square kilometers)

Boundaries Border countries: China (768 miles; 1,236 kilometers); India (1,050 miles; 1,690 kilometers); Total: 1,818 miles (2,926 kilometers)

Climate Varies, from tropical in the southern low, flat land to tundra in the northern Himalayan ranges; moist summer and dry winter, influenced primarily by monsoons

Terrain Terai or low-lying, flat river plain of Ganges in the south; hilly in the central part; and rugged and snow-capped Himalayas in the north

Elevation Extremes Contains 8 of the world's 10 highest peaks. Lowest point is Kechana Kalan, at 230 feet (70 meters); highest point is Mount Everest, at 29,035 feet (8,850 meters)

Land Use Arable land, 16.07 percent; Permanent crops, 0.85 percent (2005)

Irrigated Land 7,270 square miles (11,700 square kilometers) (2003)

Natural Hazards Severe thunderstorms, flooding, landslides, drought, and famine, depending on the timing, intensity, and duration of the summer monsoon

Natural Resources Hydropower, quartz, water, timber, scenic beauty, small deposits of lignite, copper, cobalt, iron ore, medicinal herbs

Environmental Issues Deforestation, water contamination, wildlife conservation, vehicular emissions

People

Population Total: 28.9 million; males, 14,846,870; females, 14,054,920

Population Density	407 people per square mile (157 people/square kilometer)
Population Growth Rate	2.17 percent per year
Net Migration Rate	0 migrant(s)/1,000 population
Fertility Rate	4.01 children/woman
Birth Rate	30.46 births/1,000 population
Death Rate	9.14 deaths/1,000 population
Life Expectancy	Total population: 60.56 years; males, 60.78 years; females, 60.33 years
Median Age	Total: 20.5 years; males, 20.3 years; females, 20.6 years
Ethnic Groups	Indo-Aryan, 70 percent; Tibeto-Burmese, 20 percent; other, 10 percent
Religion	Hindu, 81 percent; Buddhist, 11 percent; Muslim, 4 percent; Kirat, 4 percent; other, under 1 percent
Language	Nepali is the national and official language, spoken by 99 percent of the population. Other dominant languages: Newari, Maithili, Bhojpuri, Hindi
Literacy	(Persons age 15 and over who can read and write) Total population: 48.6 percent; male, 62.7 percent; female, 34.9 percent (2001)

Economy

Currency	Nepali rupee
GDP Purchasing Power Parity (PPP)	$41.18 billion (2006 est.)
GDP Per Capita	$1,500 (2006 est.)
Labor Force	11.11 million
Unemployment	42 percent (2004 est.)
Labor Force by Occupation	Agriculture, 76 percent; service, 18 percent; industry, 6 percent
Agricultural Products	Rice, corn, wheat, sugarcane, jute, root crops, milk, water buffalo meat
Industries	Tourism, carpet, textile; small rice, jute, sugar, and oilseed mills; cigarettes, cement and brick production
Exports	$822 million free on board (FOB); does not include unrecorded border trade with India (2005 est.)
Imports	$2 billion FOB

Leading Trade Partners	Exports: India, 67.9 percent; U.S., 11.7 percent; Germany, 4.7 percent (2006) Imports: India, 61.8 percent, China, 3.8 percent, Indonesia, 3.3 percent (2006)
Export Commodities	Carpets, clothing, leather goods, jute goods, grain
Import Commodities	Gold, machinery and equipment, petroleum products, fertilizer
Transportation	Very poorly developed. Roadways: between 10,803 miles (17,380 kilometers) and 6,143 miles (9,886 kilometers) paved. Railways: 36.6 miles (59 kilometers) paved; Airports: 47; 10 with paved runways

Government

Country Name	Kingdom of Nepal
Capital City	Kathmandu
Type of Government	Parliamentary democracy
Head of Government	Prime Minister Girija Prasad Koirala
Independence	1768 (by unification)
Administrative Divisions	5 development regions, 14 zones, 75 districts, and 3,915 Village Development Committees (VDCs)

Source: CIA, *The World Factbook* (2007)

11,000 B.C.	Evidence of the ancient life (teeth of *Rama Pithecus*) is traced to this time.
9000–8000	Evidence of Neolithic tools is traced to this time.
2500	Indus River civilization begins.
1750	Nomadic Aryans migrate into southwest Nepal.
1000	Early Hinduism begins.
563	Buddha is born; the rise of Buddhism begins.
500	The Tibeto-Burman live in Nepal.
A.D. 300–1200	The Licchavi Kingdom comes into power in Kathmandu.
1100–1484	Western Nepal is ruled by Khasa Malla kings.
1200	Ari Malla, first king of the Malla Dynasty, rules in Kathmandu Valley.
1312	Khasa king Ripu Malla leads a raid in Kathmandu Valley.
1345–1346	Sultan Shamsud-din Ilyas of Bengal raids Kathmandu Valley.
1484	The Malla Kingdom is divided into thirds; the three kingdoms of Kantipur, Bhadgoun, and Patan are established.
1559	The Gorkha Kingdom is established by Drabya Shah in western Nepal.
1606–1633	Ram Shah reigns; the Gorkha Kingdom experiences first expansion.
1742	Prithvi Narayan Shah ascends to throne of the Gorkha Kingdom.
1768	Gorkha king Prithivi Narayan Shah conquers Kathmandu, Patan, and Bhadgoun.
1769	Kathmandu becomes the capital of modern Nepal.
1775	Prithvi Narayan Shah, the first king of united Nepal, dies.
1809	Nepalese territory expands to Kangra to the west and to Teesta to the east—the farthest extent of the Gorkha Empire or Nepalese territory.

1814–1816	Anglo-British-Nepalese War is fought; the Sugauli Treaty results in the loss of Nepalese territory.
1846	Using the Kot massacre, Jung Bahadur Rana takes over as prime minister and establishes hereditary Rana rule that lasts for 103 years.
1914–1918	Thousands of Nepalese citizens fight as soldiers for Great Britain in World War I.
1923	Great Britain confirms Nepal an independent country with a friendship treaty, developing a special relationship with the British Empire.
1939–1945	Tens of thousands of Nepalese citizens fight as soldiers for Great Britain in World War II.
1947	The United States establishes diplomatic relations with Nepal.
1948	The country's first constitution, the Government of Nepal Act, is activated.
1950	The Nepali Congress Party forms, unifying other democratic parties; civil war breaks out.
1951	The Ranas fall; Mohan Shamsher becomes prime minister; the constitution is suspended.
1952	Mohan Shamsher capitulates; King Tribhuvan is restored to the throne and regains control of the army and administration; an interim constitution is enacted.
1955	King Tribhuvan dies; Mahendra ascends to the throne.
1955	Nepal is admitted to the UN.
1956	The first five-year plan of economic development is initiated.
1960	The panchayat system is launched.
1990	Democratic movement takes place; the panchayat regime falls; a multiparty democratic government is established.
1996	Maoists begin a guerrilla war.
2001	The royal massacre occurs; Prince Gyanendra Shah becomes king of Nepal.

2005 King Gyanendra dismisses the government and takes control of power.

2006 The second people's movement takes place, including seven mainstream parties and Maoists; Parliament and democratic government are reinstated; peace accord between Nepal government and Maoist guerrillas is struck; 12-year civil war ends; the government strips the king of power and status as the head of state; transition to reformed political and administrative system is achieved.

Bibliography

Cameron, M.M. *On the Edge of the Auspicious Gender and Caste in Nepal.* Chicago: Illinois University Press, 2005.

Dixit, K.M., and R. Shastri. *State of Nepal.* Kathmandu, Nepal: Himal Books, 2002.

Hachhethu, K. *The Nepali State and the Maoist Insurgency 1996–2001: Himalayan People's War, Nepal's Maoist Rebellion.* Bloomington: Indiana University Press, 2004.

Isaacson, J.M., C.A. Skerry, K. Moran, and K.M. Kalavan. *Half a Century of Development: The History of U.S. Assistance to Nepal, 1951–2001.* Kathmandu, Nepal: USAID, 2001.

Prakash, A. Raj. *"Kay Gardeko?": The Royal Massacre in Nepal.* New Delhi, India: Rupa and Co., 2001.

Shah, R. *Modern Nepal: A Political History.* New Delhi, India: Manohar Publications, 1996.

Shrestha, S H. *Economic Geography of Nepal.* Kathmandu, Nepal: Educational Publishing House, 2004.

United Nations. *Nepal 2007.* New York: United Nations, 2007.

Vaidya, T.R, T. Manandhar, and S.L. Joshi. *Social History of Nepal.* New Delhi, India: Anmol Publications, 1993.

Whelpton, J.A. *History of Nepal.* Cambridge, UK: Cambridge University Press, 2005.

Burbank, J. *Culture Shock! Nepal: A Guide to Customs and Etiquette*. Portland, Ore.: Graphic Arts Center Publishing, 1998.

Fisher, J.F. *Sherpas: Reflections on Change in Himalayan Nepal*. Berkeley: University of California Press, 1990.

Mayhew, B., J. Bindloss, and S. Armington. *Nepal*. Oakland, Calif.: Lonely Planet Publications, 2006.

Willesee, A., and M. Whittaker. *Love and Death in Kathmandu: A Strange Tale of Royal Murder*. New York: St. Martin's Press, 2004.

Web Sites

CIA World Factbook: Nepal
https://www.cia.gov/library/publications/the-world-factbook/geos/np.html

Explorersweb: Mt. Everest
http://www.mounteverest.net/

Geographia: Nepal
http://www.geographia.com/nepal/

Library of Congress Country Studies: Nepal
http://lcweb2.loc.gov/frd/cs/nptoc.html

Nepal: Central Bureau of Statistics
http://www.cbs.gov.np/

Nepal.com
http://www.nepal.com/

Nepal Government Web Site
http://www.nepalgov.gov.np/index.php

Nepal Tourism Board
http://www.welcomenepal.com/nepal/index.asp

Skyline Treks & Expeditions (cost data for mountain treks)
http://www.trekinfo.biz/expedition_royalties.php

Unleash Yourself: Nepal
http://www.welcomenepal.com/brand/index.asp

Visit Nepal.com
http://www.visitnepal.com/nepal_information/

Picture Credits

Index

energy
    hydroelectric, 29–30, 42, 81–82
    wood, 81
ethnic groups
    in hill region, 58–60
    in mountain region, 56–58
    number of, 9, 54
    See also specific peoples
Everest Marathon, 24

families
    agriculture and, 79–80
    importance of extended, 55
    importance of sons in, 55
    special deities of, 65–66
farming. *See* agriculture
festivals, 66–67, 94, 99
"Five Treasures of the Eternal Snows," 24–26
folk culture, 76–77, 85, 86
forests, 18, 81
funerals, 42, 55

Gandaki River, 29
Ganeshman Singh, 47
Gautama Buddha, 9, 12, 34
"Gem of Nepal," 103
geography
    culture and, 56
    difficulties of development and, 107
    of Kathmandu Valley, 92–93
    location, 8, 9, 10
    maps, 10, 17
    size, 9
    See also specific regions
Girija Prasad Koirala, 49, 73
"Glorious Town," 97–98
Goddess of the Harvests, 26
Gopala Dynasty, 33
Gorkha Kingdom, 36–38, 69
Gorkha soldiers (British regiment), 39, 58, 59
Gorkhapatra (newspaper), 42
government
    current, 12, 15, 105
    democratic multiparty, 49, 69, 71
    economy and, 77–78, 82, 108
    Maoists and, 15, 49–51, 70–71, 73, 106
    monarchy, 43–44, 47, 65, 68–69 (*See also specific kings*)
    party-less system of, 46–47, 68, 69
Guinness Book of World Records, 24
Gurungs, 59
Gyanendra (king), 50–51, 71, 73, 74

hill region
    climate, 28
    ethnic groups in, 58–60

Ilam District, 103
    overview of, 18–19
Hillary, Edmund P., 22, 87
Himalayas
    meaning of name, 19
    overview of, 8–9, 20
    religion and, 19, 56
    Sherpas, 22–23, 24, 27, 57–58
    tourism and, 23, 56, 57, 58, 87–89, 88–89
    World Heritage Sites in, 20–21, 23
    See also Mount Everest
Hinduism
    beliefs of, 62, 64–65
    extent of worship of, 12, 34, 56, 58, 59, 60
    gods of, 62, 64, 66
    government and, 65
    important sites to, 19, 99
    sacred texts of, 64
    See also caste system
horse soldiers, 56–57
Human Development Index (HDI), 77–78
hydroelectric power, 29–30, 42, 81–82

Ilam District, 103
India
    border shared with, 9, 14, 38
    as energy customer, 82
    independence of, 43
    threats from, 34, 35
    trade with, 47, 90
Islam, 13

Janakpur, 99
Jayasthiti Malla (king), 35–36
Jomsom, 104
Jung Bahadur Rana, 39–40, 42, 62

Kali Gandaki Gorge, 29
Kanchenjunga Conservation Area Project (KCAP), 25–26
Kanchenjunga region, 24–26
karma, 64
Kathmandu
    captured by Gorka Kingdom, 37, 69
    establishment of, 92
    general strike in, 49
    importance of religion in, 63
    overview of, 94–95
    population of, 53, 56
Kathmandu Valley
    climate, 28
    history and geography of, 92–93
    location, 19
    major ethnic groups in, 56–58
    population density in, 53

Index

About the Contributors

KRISHNA P. BHATTARAI is a native of Nepal. He currently is pursuing a master of science degree in geography at South Dakota State University. His interests and experiences lie in GIS and remote sensing. He is a visiting scientist at the USGS/EROS Data Center near Sioux Falls and a graduate teaching assistant at South Dakota State University. He holds a master's degree in geography from Tribhuvan University, Nepal, and a master of philosophy in mountain ecology from the University of Bergen, Norway.

CHARLES F. GRITZNER is distinguished professor of geography at South Dakota State University in Brookings. He is now in his fifth decade of college teaching and research. In addition to classroom instruction, he enjoys traveling, writing, working with teachers, and sharing his love of geography with readers. As a senior consulting editor for Chelsea House Publishers' *Modern World Nations* and *Major World Cultures* series, he has a wonderful opportunity to combine each of these "hobbies." Dr. Gritzner has served as both president and executive director of the National Council for Geographic Education and has received the council's highest honor, the George J. Miller Award for Distinguished Service to Geographic Education, as well as other honors from the NCGE, Association of American Geographers, and other organizations.